salmonpoetry
*Publishing Irish & International
Poetry Since 1981*

BY THE SAME AUTHOR

POETRY
Swimming Lessons
The Map of Everything
Beyond the Sea

AS EDITOR
The Colour of the World
The Compass
Uncharted Voyage
Deep Canyons

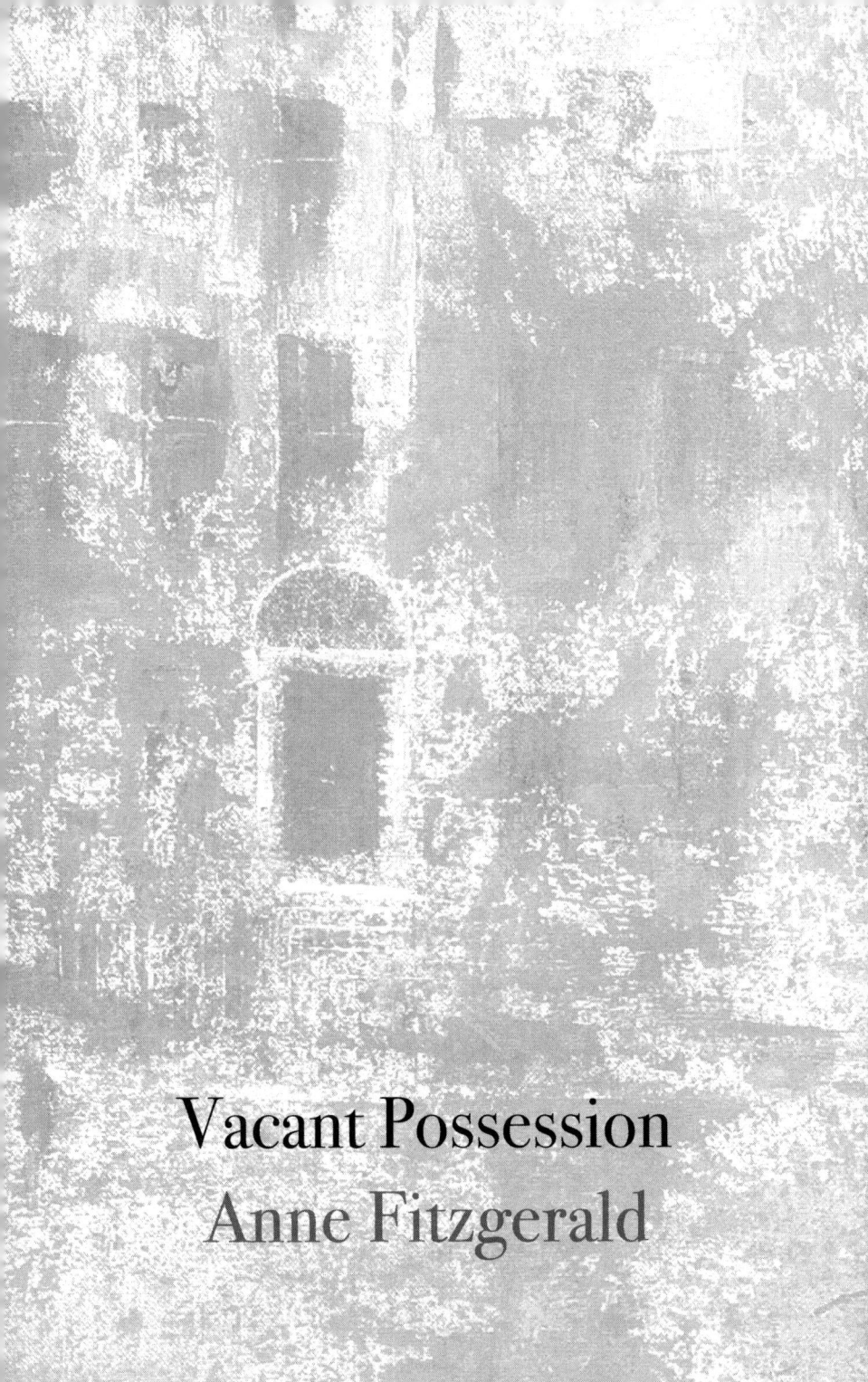

Vacant Possession
Anne Fitzgerald

First published in 2017 by
Salmon Poetry
Reprinted in 2018 by Salmon Poetry
Cliffs of Moher, County Clare, Ireland
Website: www.salmonpoetry.com
Email: info@salmonpoetry.com

Copyright © Anne Fitzgerald, 2017

ISBN 978-1-910669-97-6

The right of Anne Fitzgerald to be identified as author of this work has been asserted in accordance with Section 77 of the Copyright, Design and Patents Act 1988.

All rights reserved. No part of this publication may be reproduced or transmitted in any form or by any means, electronic or mechanical, including photography, recording, or any information storage or retrieval system, without permission in writing from the publisher. The book is sold subject to the condition that it shall not, by way of trade or otherwise, be lent, resold or otherwise circulated without the publisher's prior consent in any form of binding or cover other than that in which it is published and without a similar condition, including this condition, being imposed on the subsequent purchaser.

COVER IMAGE: *In the Rain* (1999), oil on canvas, 60 x60 cm, signed, Pearson.
Reproduced by kind permission of the artist Peter Pearson RHA.
Photograph courtesy of James Adam & Sons, Fine Art Auctioneers & Valuers.

PHOTOGRAPH: Neptune House, Temple Hill, Monkstown © Anne Fitzgerald

AUTHOR PHOTOGRAPH: © Therese Aherne

COVER DESIGN & TYPESETTING: *Siobhán Hutson*

Printed in Ireland by Sprint Print

*Salmon Poetry gratefully acknowledges the support of
The Arts Council / An Chomhairle Ealaoín*

In Memory of my beloved Parents. Journey Safely —

Annie Fitzgerald (née Aherne). June 19th, 1917 - March 28th, 2013

Charles Claffey Fitzgerald. May 20th, 1919 - July 20th, 2014

*

For Colette Murphy,
Dermot & Una McCabe.

Acknowledgements

are due to the editors for the following publications in which some of these poems or earlier versions of them first appeared:

The Battersea Review, E.ratio, Even the Daybreak: 30 Years of Salmon Poetry, The Manhattan Review, Metamorphic: 21st century poets respond to Ovid, Poetry Bus, The Recorder and *Stand Magazine.*

The poem, "Requiem for the Sold" was first broadcasted on the Ray D'arcy Show, RTÉ Radio 1, April 3rd, 2017.

I wish to thank The Palace Bar Ahernes, the Annacotty Flannerys, Mary Aherne-Ryan Cappamore and the Runnymede Ryans.

In particular I am deeply grateful to Frank McGuinness for his unwavering support throughout the years. Equally to Aidan Mathews and to Caitríona Palmer for their generous close reading of these poems, and to Peter Pearson for granting permission for his painting *In the Rain* (1999) to adorn the cover of *Vacant Possession*.

And as ever, to Jessie Lendennie and Siobhán Hutson at Salmon Poetry.

*And I saw a new heaven and a new earth:
for the first heaven and the first earth were
passed away; and there was no more sea.*

THE BOOK OF REVELATIONS: Chapter: 21:1

Contents

Introduction by Aidan Mathews   13

I

Anticipation   17
Desire   18
No Air   19
Belief in Momentary Laps   20
Blackout   21
Lost In   22
Myopic   23
Compass   24
Night Sweats   25
A Rub of the Relic   26
All Things Bright   27
Grave Digging Prospector   28
Summer   29
Over the Limit   30
Deception   31
Fields   33

II

Shingles   37
Getting Ready   39
Last Rites from My Mother   40
Tempo Rubato   42
Scent of Snowfall   44
Vacant Possession   46
Come March   56
Sauduade   57
Send Off   58
What Will Remain   59
The Little Boy from Basin Lane   61

Sibling Rivalry · 66
No Small Craft Warning · 67
Bloodline · 70
Houdini Cane · 71
Safe and Sound · 73
A Great Fall · 74
In Plain Sight · 75
Perception · 77
Prayer for My Daughter · 78

III

Éire's Holy Roman Emperor · 83
Mrs. Doogan · 86
Change of Use · 88
Making Good · 91
The Holy Land · 92
Odd Job Man · 94
The Book of Bees · 95
The Price of 1965, near Archbishop Palace · 99
Finding Myself in Werburgh Street · 101
Bellybutton · 103
A False Start · 105
Finding you at Fifty · 106
Multiplicity · 107
Districts Not Apparent · 108

IV

Requiem for the Sold · 115

Save The Child · 120

Notes on Poems	121
Selection of Sources Consulted	125
Archives	125
Books/Articles/Periodicals	125
Legislation	127
Case Law	128
Reports/Other	128
Maps	129
Newspapers	129
A Selection of Seminal Newspaper Articles	129
Private Interviews	135
Radio	135
Television/Film	137
Theatre	138
Acknowledgements	139
Author's Postscript	141
About the Author	147

Introduction

"Vacant possession", a technical term in the law of contract and conveyance, is something of a contradiction in terms, or, more primly, an oxymoron, not unlike the category of "present absentee" in the modern state of Israel. In addition, the elements of both late Latin expressions look in very different directions: the adjectives to emptiness and deprivation, the nouns to property and ownership, and the two compounds to control and/or vulnerability.

Anne Fitzgerald's poems play intently on these semantic possibilities in a threefold manner, or, if you prefer, in three trimesters of lyric poetry that conclude in the birth of a single solid volume, her fourth so far. There is the body of the self in the risk and reticence of erotic love, which begins the book, and is deeply chaste, in an old-fashioned sense. There is the body of the state, those political interlopers we call circumstance and history and the way things are (or were), which infiltrate our genealogies for better and for worse, for richer and for poorer. And there is the body of the single and the singular mother, both natural and adoptive, whose Trojan task is parturition and the ordeal of its partings, through the rule of a transcultural totem, from Christian Ireland to Islamic Indonesia, that prohibited irregular pregnancies in societies worldwide where contract and conveyance are inevitably ten tenths of the Law.

Much has been written of the latter and the last in recent times, and most of it, like most writing on most current controversies, has been opportunistic and polemical. But *Vacant Possession* is no maudlin Misery Lit. instalment in an ongoing agitprop, in part because Fitzgerald lives and moves and has her being in the Christian ecosystem of the imaginary, whose metaphors of the marginal remind us, always and everywhere, that Mary, the Venus of Nazareth, is herself the patron saint of the unmarried mother and no plaster prig on a pedestal.

Good poetry, of course, will never have the last word, because the desire to have the last word is a form of violence, and is used by victimisers posing as victims. But it will still have its quiet say as the right word spoken at the wrong time, which is the peril of its privilege. We can leave the wrong word spoken at the right time, which is the charlatan's cue, to the blockbusters.

AIDAN MATHEWS

Poet, Novelist, Dramatist
and RTÉ Radio Producer,
Palm Sunday 2017

I

*There rises an unspeakable desire
After the knowledge of our buried life*

> MATTHEW ARNOLD
> *The Buried Life*

Anticipation

From afar it comes like the smell of rain
in off the sea, with an urgency of waves
breaking, you weaken at the thought
of it happening again, as naturally as heat
making its presence felt on the globe
of your palms, you spread your fingers
wide as water between two bodies
of land, trace boundaries, sea stacks 'n' coves
on the bend of where paradise might
be. Your judgement clouds like a compass
that's let moisture in, devoid of magnetic
field you falter, give way to the rhythm
of waves as though sirens in pursuit of kelp
and driftwood like lovers on a beach.

Desire

Day need not break for you to come
into focus like a ship through fog.
You colonise my thoughts, backhandedly
like twists of fallen away wishes
to a place only darkness holds
secure in the knowledge of forethought
as if the line of a song resonating
down narrow Italian streets in pursuit
of a piazza, to lay naked my desire
for you as the sun pitches up yellow,
holds rain at bay while we figure the fall
of light across the face of the earth.
You are the a squatter who claims
vacant possession of all that is in me.

No Air

All evening I've tried to catch my breath,
a heaviness pervades. Opening windows
alleviates nothing, no breath to be caught
since that night I fell for you in ways I'd thought
not possible, over the wine we didn't spill.
You have bedded down my waking thoughts
in a slumber so deep I may never come
again to appreciate the silk lining of a kid glove,
finding fingers shape softness. And as you say
my name for the first time the taste is new
and unfamiliar. When the heat breaks,
you're still in my head, like the scent of perfume
that will not fade. In those small hours
your shadow claims the light of all that is natural.

Belief in Momentary Lapses

Somewhere between Lexington and Park
I spot you, ever before our chance encounter
at the Algonquin blossoms to obsession.

Lush with Dry Martinis and Manhattans
we relax into shadows of movement before
ice melts into the arms of intoxication.

If possession be nine tenths, it's the one just
out of reach we grasp like straws of redemption,
makes us whole again as night and day wrestle

to touch. Paper boats released from palms
set sail on the lake at Central Park
while the host is raised skyward in St. Patrick's.

Blackout

Unlike fog thickening at sea
through sounds of the horn,

you arrive unannounced.
Throw searchlights across

the hull of my heart
to a chamber you'd broke.

And like a hurricane weakened
to a tropical storm, knocking-off

traffic lights across districts,
you just up and disappear.

Lost In

Frequently I think
I'm over you,

like a moon
of mistrust

or a youth misspent,
and you come

into the frame again,
bold as brass.

Perspective tilts
middle distance

abridging those
moments unrealised.

Myopic

Too often you arrive,
spreading yourself

slowly and deliberately
across that evening

light, refusing to fade
like a child up late,

or some backwater
shade, where an orchid

flourishes. Pink bits
flower into dusk

as a life to be lived
rustles undergrowth.

Compass

Hadn't my wits about
me when I fell head

over heels. Charmed by
small refinements in

your run-on lines, leaves
words shaping my mouth

like an after taste,
guides me through a novel

terrain of soft oasis's.
I lose my sure footing

as you alter the movement
of shape, slow motion up.

I stumble under the weight
of your magnetic field.

Night Sweats

You have taken
my sleep away

to a far off place.
A distant land

where dreams run
riot. Broad brush

strokes can not
hide action beneath,

like characters
waiting to be drawn,

entangles the lining
of my thoughts

in each breath,
strips hues from pigments,

exposes buds of love
frost bitten with desire

you have left aside,
for another to flower.

A Rub of the Relic

It was there in Whitefriar Street
Church I genuflected at the heart

of St. Valentine's Shrine on the feast
of lovers, having come from Holles

Street, to light candles for biopsies
a gynaecologist took. Tongues

smart like the wall of my womb
bright as d'bunch of roses peeking

from a fellow in the front pew, lost
in prayer, looks for love amongst

sacraments and reliquary, covets
his neighbour's wife, sat between

third and fourth Stations.
She focuses on the tabernacle

opening up as if the first
fair crocus of Spring.

All Things Bright

Trouble with Joey White was never
straight forward, finds pleasure in
pulling wings off bluebottles whilst
sporting a rabbit's foot about his neck.
He'd a hard neck, Nora Devine says,
pulling pints at Cappamore horse fair,
between local jams and tractor stands,
keeps *Arthur* fast flowing and Joey
on the ball as he shoots plastic ducks
in combat with his own Afghanistan
funfair. Not unlike the night he makes
the sun rise in Kennedy's hay barn
as if dawn breaking the horizon below
a 747 belly, above cauliflower clouds.

Grave Digging Prospector

Neither safe sex nor religion does
John-Joe practice, hankers more
after the scent of rain on dry earth.
For pink adventures earthworms
might have or rough terrain ladybirds
traverse as the moon negotiates
its phases John-Joe looks for one
who has a touch of the liver fluke
about them. Open to his tomfoolery
of panning for gold in mud, water
has left, says it be nuggets he's after,
body of carats that intrigues,
like the contours of cupid's bow above
Joseph Mary Martin's hair-lip
dug out of a face fit for a Grecian urn.

Summer

The moon lies high tonight caught
in summer stillness holding its breath
as we do at Peggy Guggenheim's
imagined party, where Dick Murphy
fancies himself as F. Scott, decked out
in an off-white three piece from Burtons
and his Zelda, a haberdasheries delight
kitted out in all kinds. Down they goes
to the river, punt across its surface, see
reeds hug the heal of their hull as the world
turns downside up: clouds float on water's
skin, a gadfly hangs its head like a child
chastised, clouds roll by small movements
in bull rushes out past the memory of heat.

Over the Limit

Long for it to pass when
Leafy Devine seeks redress

for claims of apodyopsis
levelled against him last

Thursday week in young
Matthew Sweeney's snug

over *Advocaat* and cheap
communion wine, washed

down by fingers of sherry
brought back from a fling

in Porto. Where this claim
was the order of the day

round with possibilities
after a small plethora of

Crème de Menthe Frappés,
leaves Leafy Devine with

a bit of a thing for green.
Grows he does, fistfuls

of grass in his fridge, prays
to penicillin bread, sports

'n' curls butter into whorls
surfers be proud of as he

builds a wild Atlantic wave
inside the body of his Bosch.

Deception

Never before is
the likes of it seen.

Lar Thatcher hanging
as if some strange fruit

from Ducky Tibbett's
yew, counting woodworm

holes they says,
looking for the soul

of wood, where
the curl of whorls

knot memory
growing skyward

the night before
he's cut to size.

Mushroom pickers
are lovers in disguise

as if drunks who
set fire to trunks,

warm their affections
in dawn's hollow

pockets, appears trivial
in light of Lar's shadow

cast like a fly fisher
where the play

of colour attracts
fish to death

in the reeling in
and letting go.

Fields

Little by little big things happen.
Joey Finch let loose secrets

as if nuggets from the Klondike
at Kennedy's kitchen table.

Marty Duignan two fields over
releases hens 'n' chickens in sight
of foxes under lunar pathways.

Geese take redeye flights of fancy
across drills of sleeping beetroots.

And nearby Ellen Rowland's Holy
Well comes a crying, as a new damp

rag is tied to a prayer tree above
the Mulkear, heading for the Shannon.

II

After the first death, there is no other.

DYLAN THOMAS
*A Refusal to Mourn,
the Death by Fire of a Child in London*

Shingles

At the end
of the ward

light makes free
with your forgotten

pattern of memory
as if brail hidden

in sunlight
hits the heart

of St. Bridget's
Cross above

your head.
Celtic reeds

read
your thoughts

as Saints 'n'
Souls hover.

You enter
a delirium

of white
washed walls

baby blue
hydrangeas

sway
to cow-tail

face-slaps
dawn milking

as Ramsey Hunt
syndrome roams,

covets optic nerve,
defaces your beauty

in burn scars
and vanity scabs

as you rave of pots
boiling over.

What's for dinner?
I'm not eating.

Look how
I've been left.

You'll take me?
We'll get the bus

home
to Camden Street?

Does my mother
know where I am?

Getting Ready

Go to *Shaws* for white sheets,
Egyptian cotton, a high thread

count mind, to lay me out.
Use candles in that bottom

drawer, John XX111 thrice
blessed, making a bishop

of Tom Ryan back in '63.
Light them so I will find

my way through d'eye
of the needle, ease tight

squeeze, deaden clamouring
at the gates. Let me pass

without incident for what
I have left unresolved.

Last Rites from my Mother

Already your scent
has disappeared

          I won't please you
          to go in a hurry.

with the sound
of your voice,

          Is my Mother alive?
          That's terrible.

or the way you'd
cut and core apples

          Is she really dead?
          You'll have to get

for a tart, of how
your thumbprint

          used to that. I've taught
          you everything I know.

would remain
on pastry rolled out

          There's nothing more
          I can tell you about only,

with a milk bottle
baked on a dinner plate

          I'm going on
          a journey shortly.

aerated with fork
prongs of release.

          I'll be leaving soon,
          to meet my Mother.

The scent of hairspray,
to hold your fine hair

                                    I don't know where.
                                    Am I dead?
let go grey, of how
you'd never be early
                                    You will have
                                    to let me go. Know,

for mass, in before
the gospel would do.
                                    I've loved you always,
                                    and forever, the best of all.

Tempo Rubato

Pulling on travel
socks before take

off transports me
to your nursing home

room, where I take
flight with you for ten

of your last twelve nights.
Sleeping upright on

a chair, holding your hand
for fear of letting go

as your mind unravels
its black box to dances

in Rearcross, freewheeling
past bracken by a stream

chickens, and the lamb
you reared with calves,

and the lamb of God
that will not take away

the soul of our sins.
Not two fields over

from the fellow who
shot Collins fell.

His blood they say
stains grass still.

A bald patch where
green refuses to grow.

A bit like my belief
you'll not pull through

telling me in the dead
of your tenth night

My Life is Over —
as you battle for breath

oxygen nebulises
the small hours in vain.

Turbulence disturbs
your flight path home

breaks dawn over Dublin
mountains, might well

be the Sheanafork or Moher Clé.
Snow that cannot take, falls.

When whiteness does hold
the world as I know it is no more.

Scent of Snowfall

For too long now
the absence of rain

clouds opinion
blossoming your baby

pink arguments
in full flight, blows

proportion out
of sight like a kite

that's lost flight.
You journey back

a life in six
months, each hour

protracts a refined indignity
reserved for scientists

to pour over
as time spills unevenly

through new zones,
throws reason over

for a logic of delirium
houses small phrases

from three quarters
of a century ago

pearls of wisdom
saved in clarity

like the night
heaven opens

to receive
your soul

snow falls.
A blizzard

of disbelief
whitens my

world as
I knew it.

Vacant Possession

> In Memory of My Mother,
> Annie Fitzgerald (née Aherne)

i. *The Home Place*

Within the barony
of Oweney and Arra

in the Archdiocese
of Cashel and Emly,

in the parish of Kilcommon,
Hollyford and Rearcross,

about two miles on
from the Long Stone,

above in Foilduff, deep
amongst overgrown lushness,

an Amazonian leafiness
breaks through the heart

of ground, between walls
without roof, sky-touches

a green longing, not seen
since four brothers walk

down this aisle
of rhododendrons

to Limerick
for Dublin trains

one after another
like the speed of their births.

Ajar, late afternoon enters
your front door, as if

Black and Tans, spreads
itself out, exposes layers

of magnolias and apricots
beneath wood panelling.

Paint remains in
the absence of family

like a secret festering,
thrives under rain.

Heart's tongue soars
over moss, brambles

and briars claim
enforcement

like the Land
Commission's

relocation policy,
flings a locked

chain over shoulders
of a cattle gate,

a *Sanctuary,*
Land Preserved,

sign, hangs
from its neck

like the weigh
of a forgotten parish

well below
Keeper Hill.

ii. *My Grandmother*

In 1914 your hand pulls
a calf from its mother

as the Black Hand pulls
the world into war

shooting Archduke
Franz Ferdinand

in Sarajevo, puts off
partition, passes

the third home rule
act as the IRB revolt

five years before
the father of your

five sons and two
daughters is gifted

a horse-kick death
two years after

Ma-Breen pulls
your last, Annie,

into a world where
eldest son Patrick

gets Foilduff,
trades it for Fethard

after a spell.
You leave the land

in the wake
of four Dublin bound

sons, who serve
time behind bars

in Camden, Cork
and Park Gate Streets

before pulling pints
behind their own counters.

Above in Temple Bar,
you begin again

with Annie, who
marries Charlie in 1949.

Chicken replaces turkey
on the twenty-fifth

as a birdsong of drunks
break dawn in this city

on the brink.
Behan looks for money

back on empties.
Unions strong-arm

a barmen strike,
helps move you all

from this slum in 1960
to the Victorian seaside

of Sandycove where
you will thrive till

snow falls on
Buffinokio and Lackabeg

as a barn owl kills
the Foilduff dead

of night and your
breath above in Sandycove.

Snow stills January
third, Nineteen Sixty Five.

   iii. *My Mother*

From a five-bar
gate you'd swing

to and fro the day,
shy faced and hint

of ginger curl,
in calico smock

and knee stocks
hid in brown boots

passed down,
whose souls stud

hills and streams,
to school, horse fairs,

and dancehalls. Clip
clop of pony and trap

to mass of a Sunday
from Foilduff-Jackson

to Rearcross, stopping
at Flannery's for a few

bits on tic, as the Railway
clock tick-tock's your hearth,

warms griddle cakes
after gospel sermon.

Having learned Mrs Carey's
long division and to read

(her husband they say read
big ship upside down at sea

for the Lusitania sinking,
reads no print, only pictures).

To Toor secondary you'd
not go, to learn Shakespeare

or seabirds of the British Isles
but perfect instead a lightness

of touch, baking sponge buns
with butterfly wings, a dab

hand at white washing the sum
of the square of the hypotenuse

o' walls, and the other two sides
of turning milk into cheese nay

mention, stray theorems in
between the creation of hay

cocks in fields as hillocks
o' hope like cities on a map.

Toomevara, Borrisoleigh
Limerick junction, Dublin.

iv. *Local Activity, 1920*

On the road to Newport
cycling to Petty Sessions

from Rearcross barracks
constables, Finn, McCarthy

and Byrne are set upon
by twenty scarecrows,

posing as armed men
at Lackamore, above

your birthplace
Lackabeg.

Finn and McCarthy fall.
Byrne's takes a share

of slugs. Mounts
his cycle to Newport.

Raises the alarm.
No arrests made.

What of the night
the RIC barracks

burnt to the ground
beside Flannery's shop?

Stars fall on heads
that would not roll

like silent thunder
rumbling countryside

ditches where pikes
and guns sleep-tight.

v.

Black and Tans strip
Towerhill's roof for lead.

Leads to bullets finding
homes in the queerest

of folk and tomfoolery
in outhouse distilleries,

alerts local constabulary
of movements inside on

cycling by, asses
braying in a field.

vi.

Foilduff's Amazonian
lushness runs

through my head like
the boundary

of a relic in
need of touch,

rooted in old
red sandstone

with a high virgin
blanket of peat

and poor fertility.
It's a wonder how

a widow raises
seven children on

the side of Moher Clé
between world wars.

vii.

Windthrow hinders
crop stability

as the Mulkear rises
in Glenduff, runs

through Foilduff,
Foilduff Jackson

Coumnagillagh,
Baurnadomeeny,

Laghile, Goulmore,
Coonmore and Foildarragh.

Shaping landscape
and deer running free.

Come March

Fists of magnolia
loosen Winter's grip.

A falling away occurs
like conversations petering

out, face belts of Spring
breezes, folding and unfolding

white petals, not unlike
the sheet I shake creases

from to spread over
your body after

you've gone
with wind and rain.

Saudade

And as you slip away love pours out
of us like a river making for the sea,
passing through the straits of grief
and sadness to that unmapped country
of carrying on. Fighting like brothers
and sister over who said what, aimlessly
trying to bring you back, as your small
gestures of kindness become big details
in the nowness we flounder through.
Geraniums on the windowsill catch
evening photosynthesising, spreads
itself across the body of mahogany
dining room table as if the Atlantic.
Rays light up family photographs
on the mantle like could-be Broadway
icons facing just west of happiness.
So, where does all our love go after
you have gone, back over the mountain
and downhill to the scent of sea.

Send Off

In a black suit, baby pink blouse
onyx 'n' pearls about neck and ears

you're dressed for Charon, with penny
in pocket for safe passage to the other

side, after your breath leaves its soul
to its own devices. Where do you go

as we lower you, on straps that would
hold a piano in a truck, unlike tunes

you could not, slipping into sleep
singing *Show Me the Way to go Home*.

When I do go home after mourners
are fed, an emptiness triangulates

the memory your touch leaves
tucking you in to bed, you'd say

don't close the door, it's like a coffin.
I want to see the light of heaven.

From your lunar aspect, you shine
the light of heaven down on me.

What Will Remain

In Glasthule and Greystones
shades of you survive —
in pink and green recycling bins.

Brown shoes you walked me to school
in. My hand in yours up the stairs
to Miss Murray's table of pedagogy.

Black gloves 'n' mantilla sported
at Tom Ryan's ordination under
a Roman sun. A mitre for Clonfert

Bloomsday 1963, amidst a sea of hats,
would-be Fellini extras later
listen to their bishop and the Nightie

affair over airwaves, like shame
of a girl in the family way caught
boarding Dún Laoghaire's Mail Boat.

Or a black suit you would have worn
to Michael Cleary's funeral, before it broke
he'd fathered two sons. *A lovely priest,*

gave a great retreat in the parish, you'd said
and a few quid to his missions, could scarcely
believe, after d'Casey affair 'n' Gay Byrne's

refusal to shake Annie Murphy's hand
on telly. Still your faith did not waver.
Women must be to blame sure look at Eve

and the damage she caused with an apple.
Couldn't be possible for a holy man to act
like they're saying, he's be all about God

not power puffs, silk stockings and lipsticks.
His fingers be caught in rosary beads not small
female spaces, but know mostly smoothness

of bible leaves fingering the turn of gospels
as if thighs. Shame on those who belittle
the holy See having beat tables into children.

Only following a pure trail of frankincense
and communion wine. No Havana circle
a royal flush going down like a hand of regret.

Forget me not and do this in memory of me
pierce hosts like sunlight though stained glass.
No angles sing …*suffer little children* at Temple

Hill, its gates now open for business again.
Estate agents point out architectural features
saved from this Georgian House, nuns sold

babies from. Top dollar for posh seaside
apartments. Partition walls cordon off
stripped paint, crayon marks and live wires

gone dead from lack of love. High ceilings
let light from the sea dominate asking prices.
Fair winds blow nuns neglect of what

happened into the small hours. Cavity walls
hold cries no insulation will soundproof,
trying to escape only proves to be in vain.

McQuaid's the man. Saved thousands of little
souls from Protestantism. Curious his ethos still
runs through all arteries of our body politic.

The Little Boy from Basin Lane

    i

Where James Street cuts
 Basin Lane you are born

between Wars, after
the Treaty of Versailles,

long after posh
people come to take

the air. Coaches drive
through an archway

fit for Pharaohs
as the river Poddle

Back of the Pipes draws
them to water-acres.

Over five and one-quarter
English acres, all class

of orchestral music
is heard play in Pig Town.

ii

Instead of counting sheep
we say the Alphabet, turning

back hospital bedsheets.
Charles circles your wrist.

Named after an uncle who
went for messages, never

came back. Joined British
Army, letters say later.

Barrels roll cobbles, tip o' toe
from James' Gate to barges

at the Grand Canal. Guinness
bound for Porter Houses far

and near under city air
pregnant with hops.

You left Synge Street
aged twelve 'n' a cleverer

little boy with words
from your Lane, *wrote*

poems after. Kinsella
is his name. Thomas.

iii

Mammy would be so proud
of me. The little boy from Basin Lane.
I served mass religiously
in John's Lane, ran from d'chance
of placing pennies on the Dead
at uncle Claffey's undertakers
yard on Usher's Island. Instead
to O'Neill's of Camden Street I go.
From its top window is where
I first sees your beautiful Mother
'n' again in Aherne's. She serves
me a pint and sixty-four years
between Temple Bar and Sandycove
where we flourish and prosper.

iv

Mammy would be so proud
of me. The little boy from Basin Lane.
If she could have seen Sandycove
with Charles Fitzgerald over the door.
A redbrick Victorian landmark
for actors, fly-fisher-Judges, writers,
painters 'n' punters to share balls
of malt, whackers 'n' fingers of port
till closing time. I entertained no
afterhours, cards nor singing. I ran
an honest Lounge-Bar with St. Martin
of Tours collection box chained
to the countertop like a pilgrim
on the road to Santiago de Compostela.

v

On the Sisters of Charity
Fifty acres at Elm Park

surrounded by strangers
and indignity the lack

of privacy brings
to a world you can bear

no more, you acquiesce.
Before the Shipping News

broadcasts you die
in a Public ward.

The Little Boy
from Basin Lane who

makes good, departs
almost with as much

you were born into.
And a blind belief

in things you
chose not to see.

Sibling Rivalry

Fourteen months after our Mother
opens the ground to lead the way,

we give our Father back to her
beneath July's hot dark dry soil.

And not twenty-four hours after
it begins afresh, that rumbling Vesuvius.

Hidden in small unsuitable gifts
over the years, pent up resentments

tight as fists, throw insults to air
as a sour pettiness matures like wood-fired

oak over who got more hugs or extra
scoops of ice cream, who was loved most

and who loved more, in a home where
a demonstrative hand was slow to show.

No Small Craft Warning

> And whoever was not found written
> in the book of life was cast
> into the lake of fire.
> — REVELATIONS Ch: 20. 15.

i

Viking, North Utsire, South Utsire,
Forties, Cromarty, Forth Tyne,

Dogger, Fisher, German Bight,
declare their positions four times

a day, ours remains less obvious.
Humber, Thames, Dover, Portland.

Our holy family clusters fourteen
months after Mother for Father's

final lift. Watch pine settle upon pine
in the absence of rain beneath belief.

Plymouth, Biscay, Trafalgar,
FitzRoy, Sole, Lundy, Fastnet.

Prayers fall into dugout earth, receives
their souls into the hands of each other.

Wind easterly, cyclonic at times.
Visibility poor. Shannon, Rockhall,

Malin, Bailey, Fair Isle, Faeroes,
Southeast Iceland. Rough fog patches.

A small craft warning to fishermen
in Plymouth and Yarmouth issues.

ii

In tongues no apostle could fathom
arguments thrive till the Red Sea parts

for a second time. Moses holds no
staff out over water throughout nights

strong east winds divide the sea
of things we do not talk of. No Song

o' the Sea is heard. No pillar of cloud
or fire to guide. No Sistine Chapel-like

fresco adorns blood red walls in Glasthule
parish church, but Imogen Stuart's bronze

Tree of Life sculpture, we are not written
in. Stories of Exodus and Passover, biblical

flights and wandering the desert in search
o' the promised land, like a mythical abyss

of *The Waltons* mourners cast upon us,
believe we are hermetically sealed by grief,

as *It's a Long Way to Tipperary* carries
our Mother out through crowds blocking

sunlight, in the wake of frankincense.
To burn again fourteen months later up

the same aisle as our Father dreamt
he dwelt in Marble Halls. Melodies run

in our heads like marbles waiting
to kiss the harmony of discord.

Low Fisher 1007 expected Norway
1002 by 0600 tomorrow. Low 150 miles

northeast of Faeroes 1003 expected
just northeast of Fair Isle with little

change by same time.
Low Tyne 1006 losing its identity.

Bloodline

Thing is, we have
the measure
of one and other.

In certain lights you
can see it, like
a doubt questioning

what is known.
That slight resemblance
unmoors balance

suggests rumours
of otherness
for ease of saving face.

Houdini Cain

> The opposite of love is not hate, it's indifference.
> —Eli Wiesel

i

Shortly after my First Communion, before
the age of reason, Houdini Cain gives again
his word: he'll treat me, after loads of broken
promises, to a day at the Pictures or Duffy's Circus.

All morning I wait by a window for Cain to turn
the corner back from the night before he took
twenty-eight Lady Laverys from the safe belly

of my piggy-bank, cousin Mary brought back
from Kentucky or Kanturk, an exotic turquoise
little fellow sports a pink flower by its ear gone

deaf from shock of Cain's fingers rooting at
a fiver's refusal to come clean out of its snout,
so he offers it to the floor, '...*I've to get the first
round 'n' play my hand in Finnegan's back bar...*'

on his knees picks up my small Communion coins
like a beggar who's spilt his cup. Afterwards
the room wheels with a stillness as if before dawn.

ii

Harbour Hotel and *Dear Frankie* keep us company
over bacon and cabbage. Steam kills our view
of Howth from the kitchen window. Between hail

showers and One O'Clock News Cain's late return
for our day, sees us tear up the road in his Fiat 127,
like Evil Knievel owes money. Beyond Glenageary

bridge we make for Ballybrack, past Charlie McQuaid's
Notre Dame des Bois on Military road, to *The Igo Inn*,
our Circus Animal Desertion. After ten green bottles

of 7*UP*, I gets fed up and pine for home, as Cain holds
court at the bar, buys jar for fellows he has just met,
lets a stranger pick me up my ears for a bet, till I cry.

He places the last of my communion money on a sure
thing that's pipped at the post. Pickled eggs races hold
sway with punters for pints of *McArdles*, and a goldfish

for good measure. *Kiskadee* and *Babycham* girls
throw keys in ashtrays and small change in black-baby
boxes, a fellow from *Notre Dame des Bois* collects

between Good Friday lock-in and the Resurrection.
Before condoms sell in toilets, or holes in the wall
give cash, McQuaid's man in Killiney does d'rounds

ensures no bar fly consorts with West-Brits even
for *King Crisps*. I burst with boredom building beer
-mat castles a drunk breaches...*Show Me the Way*

*to go Home... I had a little drink about an hour ago
'n' it's gone right to...* his head. Cain's 127 weaves hills
home, strikes up his favourite lullaby to me, a love

song of sorts ... *was an old woman in the woods...down
by* The River Saile... *she stuck a penknife in the baby's
heart...Weila, Weila, Waile,...down by* The River Saile...

Safe and Sound

is what you said we would
be, when it comes to light.

There's not much to it all
in the end. Consider, hulls

ripped by rocks, lungs fill
up, seagulls circle a split skiff.

A Great Fall

Was not much
more than twenty

four hours, for us
to come asunder

after our parents left
us for holy God.

All the king's horses
and all the kings men

can never put us
together again.

In Plain Sight

i

Once, Mother was in
hospital having teeth out.

*Look through its round
centre* you had said, *see*

the world anew as you
hand me a *Spangle*

and later, my first pair
of *Levis*, followed

by years of see-through
glass gift-things.

Hard to fathom how
your deception hid

so silent, beautiful
and neat in simple

lack of love
for transparency.

ii

Where did the boy
go who kept vigil

with Dad over
me, after doctor Boland

said, *she could die
in the night, watch over*

her till first light. You
and Dad like archangels

guide my turbulent
breathing into small hours

with prayers 'n' *Lucozade*.
I sleep upright for fear

my lungs will drown
or I'll choke on a cough

as pneumonia revisits,
to take no firm hold.

Vicks nebulises till dawn
claims day and medicine

kicks to touch. Hard
to credit, your kindness

as a young man
dissolved to harden

into something else
altogether, just out of reach

not unlike Mother's
solitaire looking up

to me. Clear-eyed. Proud
in its refined integrity.

Perception

Often you'd see it before dawn
spreading itself across the body

of Scotsman's Bay. Before Howth
rises as a mountain or Rennie's arms

emerge as a Pier, an egret perches
at Elephant Rock. The cusp of day

separates as a watercolourist
wash, diffuses pentimento despite

chiaroscuro's honest treatment
of light, as if a shadow on a lung

or the horizon drawing its line.
Colour breaks land from sea,

unmoors natural laws,
shipwrecks beneath, skull

and crossbones above
our Father's Crucifix he thumbs

at Glorious Mysteries.
Beads he will pass down

not unlike the Turin Shroud.
Word is according to the street.

Prayer for my Daughter

After I am gone take
that small cardboard

box from Foilduff,
full of family and friends

down to Sandycove.
Step into a skiff,

row out past
Victorian Baths

into Scotsman's Bay
until parallel

with Ballyghein
'n' Burdett Avenues.

Find the gap we used
see red sails from

our kitchen window
and there drop anchor.

Pull oars in
lay them across

one another
as pallbearer's

hands in prayer.
Steady your spirit level,

stand like a Eucharist
Minister. From the hull's

heart hold my box
chalice-like, give memorial

cards to fish
as if flies, photographs

cut to size, made fit
around *mother of mercy*

pray for us, squared by
indulgences shipwrecked.

Tides will read their paper
headstones, will watermark

betrayals across faces
cast from familial folklore

to the annals
like Commandments

if Howth is Mount Sinai
Kingstown Pier is the Failed Bridge.

III

There is no haystack so large that the needle in it cannot be found. But it takes time, it takes humility and a serious reason for searching.

WILLIAM MAXWELL
Time With Darken It

Éire's Holy Roman Emperor

i

At Muriel J. Gallagher's birthing house
mid-wives Farrell and Hickey drop babies

off for Neptune House at Temple Hill.
Sr. Xavier pulls up in a Hillman, picks

dodgy birth certificates up with baba's
attached, for their sale of work. Eeny will

go as the crow flies to Spiddal. Meeny,
to haberdashers in their fifties. Miney will

settle for less than a share of goodwill
and Moe will go from pillar to post, finding

no faith in human nature, peace on earth
nor land to roam free where McCormack's

Long Way to Tipperary is a hallowed creed
in little god, Charlie McQuaid's world.

ii

To *Ashurst*, McQuaid will go, as McCormack
departs. Twelve acres on Military road

Killiney, he renames as *Notre Dame des Bois*.
Primate of all Ireland sports the Borgia ring.

On their knees devotees kiss his blessed
talisman, he rubs through thick and thin

of Teacher's and Barman's strikes he fixes
with the aplomb of a 1951 Pink Gin. Unlike

Noël Browne's Mother and Baby Scheme,
McQuaid fights tooth 'n' nail, as if Machiavelli

in the Colosseum. His baby trade remains
intact unlike the hymens of girls others make

free with, sent by religious orders to help out,
when not servicing their own depraved desires.

iii

Leaving *Notre Dame des Bois*, McQuaid's
Humber draws up past many a corner boy.

In the Mail Boat's wake, he wonders are Mothers
with Child aboard he'll lose to the Mainland.

He passes his cash-cow holding-pen Temple
Hill, calculates price of little heads on the road

to his Drumcondra Palace. Babies lie idly in
rows of cots studying Osborne's stucco work,

leaves a love of perspective and a rage for order
in them, he flings them to the four corners

at a whim. Each night his pupil dilates through
an artificial lens of his telescope, traces Orion

and skinny dippers on Killiney beach brace cold
as Vatican II loosens its grip and his from Sr. Denis.

iv

Seated at his right hand in *Notre Dame des Bois*
Sr. Denis opens doors, lights fires, serves his meals

and the nation for *arrangements made* that'll rock
Éire's cradle for generations. Into baby-blue lined

ledgers she commends given-up names in lieu
of small considerations. Puts Mason and Dixon

to shame. Breathes new life into arterial roads,
mountain ranges, baronies and parishes cartographers

had all but forgotten, with off-spring from unmarried
to married. Sr. Denis draws lines under lives that might

have been. Lays Éire's Holy Roman Emperor out
in Seventy-Three. Pious processions pay their respects

to a slight Cavan man a mitre made tall, decked out
like a Borgia. His reign reaches beyond Ptolemy's

foresight, becomes the pentimento of Irish weather
systems moving over a landscape that allows no change.

Mrs. Doogan

Off to Knock, or Lough Derg
at the drop of a hat she'd run.

The Pied Piper had nothing on
her, what with her direct line

to McQuaid, nuns would phone.
Sr. Aloysius here, I've another.

Collect her from Kingsbridge.
Eve is due soon, a recidivist, at that.

Over green fields and stone walls
Eve comes, to be beside the seaside

as her belly grows hard in consideration
of light housework, collects Doogan's

brats 'n' blatherwrack for the rose garden
McQuaid planted out front, till she comes

full term. Afterwards, for a few quid
more, Doogan leaves Eve's day-old baby

in Temple Hill. Every All Soul's, two
hundred Lady Laverys appear in Doogan's

palm like footed turf, from his Grace
for her to do-good, as she sees fit

with proceeds of two babas bound
for Amerikay, she spreads among parish

Legion of Mary's and ne'er-do-wellers.
Kick-backs from the Bird's Nest,

Cottage Home and Temple Hill funds
her Lourdes trips, a plethora of plenary

indulgences and a cache of holy water
naggins, sporting St. Jude medals,

she gives as keepsakes to girls taken
in, in lieu of babies she'd helped sell on.

Change of Use

i

If Neptune be the marriage of Heaven
and Earth and McQuaid God's man

on the ground, then Neptune House is home
for his deep rooted sleight of hand, populating

the Earl of Clonmel, aka Copper Face Jacks,
Georgian hideaway at Temple Hill, with little

children born of women without men to bind
them in the bands of holy matrimony, at sea

in a world of illegitimacy saved by life-buoy
McQuaid. With his eye on the main chance

J.C. sends in the Sisters of Charity to usurp
M.J. Cruice's abode for fallen girls, creates

St. Patrick's Guild and Infant Hospital, prices
each child's head, surer odds than McGrath's

Irish Sweepstakes. Behind granite walls, tall
trees hide McQuaid's domestic export industry

in plain sight at seaside suburbia. Neighbours
twitch net curtains but appear not to ask why

people come 'n' go, by foot and Mercedes Benz
in and out of high closed gates at Temple Hill.

ii

Below the Virgin Mary, Sr. in-Charge writes
make-believe stuff up on babies files. Mixes

lies in truth as if snow-globes shaken, ensures
truth-flakes will not rise as nuns keep Mum. *In*

Excelsis Deo over knowledge to rights of blind
alleys they create, like slow burning incendiary

devices. Easier trace origins of Moore St. *Outspans*
than birth Saturn and Ops whose offspring stare up

at Patrick Osborne's plasterwork from row
upon row of iron cots, as if chickens in coops.

Their little arms stretch out to touch a ceiling rose
two horses high, or hope for hands to lift them up

leaves a remoteness that stills their inner lives.
Instils distrust as Doctors-in-Charge inject trial

drugs into legs that have yet to walk. To advance
medicine, in-camera investigations will say later.

iii

After months or years of basic care, picked up
when necessary, left out in rain to study the fall

of drops amongst apple blossoms gone pale, or
follow cloud movements to the death of sunshine.

Gravel is raked. Daffodils yellow. Cars pull up
amidst footsteps and talk across polished floors.

Parlour doors open. Well-to-do couples leave
donations with Sisters of Charity for infant-in-arms.

Ball-park, seventy to a hundred thousand punts, babies
bound for Amerikay, less Lady Laverys grease palms

if left in the Republic. McQuaid's handmaiden's file
no tax returns if sent to Tallahassee or Termonfeckin.

Little people whose antecedents will battle nature
versus nurture till kingdom come for arrangements

made. Commended into hands who will fail to shake
true nature from souls that refuse to be given up.

Making Good

We strip the Christmas table cloth
of condiments, in a waltz-like

fashion move towards each other,
ears of my corners to yours as though

straining for a harpsichords note
to fall. There it is, between thumb

and index, a faint blue-purple tinge
of veins, two Z's intertwined with

a number along its side. I'd spotted
it after wine spilt on brandy butter

you'd think a mortal sin occurred
till you pipe up, *the Swastika Laundry.*

*Sr. Denis swears by them, they've ways
to get any stain out others don't.*

*Our watermark will be right as rain.
Top hotels send stuff to them, even*

the Archbishop himself lets his
sheets be touched by little laundress

hands, washing clean original sin
like the confessional where a world

made flesh is absolved of all petty
misdemeanours and future allegations.

The Holy Land

> I go, and it is done. The bell invites me. Hear it not, Duncan
> for it is the knell that summons thee to heaven, or to hell.
>
> Macbeth – Act 2, scene 1, lines 3.

i

Get your coat we're off to The Holy Land.
Sr. Denis rang, Come up now. J.C. is in Rome
on church business, my Mother says.

From Sandycove we make for the Vico, turn right
onto Military Road to Notre Dame des Bois.
Driving through J.C. McQuaid's gates, twelve acres hide

from his flock behind red-brick Victorian walls,
a chauffeur's lodge and gravel driveway by a lawn
big as St. Peter's, with our Lady on a sea of grass.

Beyond cover of horse chestnuts, turrets and belfry
loom. The Pro-Cathedral pales into insignificance
as McQuaid's Gothic Castel Gandolfo fills our eyes.

Sr. Denis beckons us to the oak front door, *park*
the Merc under eucalyptus shade. Placing her palm
on my crown we enter, light sash windows allow

flood this parquet ocean we walk upon. Its memory
inlaid, like talk caught in one of his thirteen
bedrooms. A mahogany pod-table sports Lily o' Valley

as if the Kish. Signals panel walls 'n' escutcheons shy
of day under Christmas cake plasterwork where
McQuaid pens the Adoption Bill, (Dev passes in 1952),

beneath his grand staircase we brush by to woodland
and lawn out back, deep as the Forty Foot. Over Earl Grey
'n' Marietta's I count twenty odd trefoil windows,

plucking the Archbishop's daises for chains we wear
as Mum and Sr. Denis trace Ahernes of Foilduff 'n' Rearcross
and its tin church that sailed all the way from Wales.

ii

Down by the walled garden we pick J. C.'s apples.
A cock crows near his hen run Sr. Denis lifts eggs
from, saying, *Let's fly to see holy God before you go.*

To the belfry-lift Peter Pence built we head. Cut sky
blue-open as we rise above canopy of elms and rooftops.
Amalfi dominates through Irelands Eye, McQuaid's

telescopic peephole. His Holy See amidst a Freemasons
enclave. Knights of Columbanus, Legion of Mary's
thumbing sorrowful mysteries to those that got away.

Latin chants still haunt as priests turn their backs
on congregations, a fear of not seen drop
enough money into collections, hear gossip break

ground. See secrets sear respectability, mass stipends
take money from pockets and bread off tables, while waves
of lovers fuel his baby trade like swimmers wading out

to sea. From belfry deck McQuaid's hammer strikes
the Angelus across his little Vatican, our ears ringing
like parishes rebelling, we descend Dantesque as if

the weight of water falling back into its baptismal font,
fingers snug in our ears, half drowns the summons to prayer
in his aspic world made flesh for a red hat he'll not get.

Odd Job Man

Nuns give John-Joe a start
tightening screws on cots.

His calling is in damaged
things. Through his hands

they pass like the word
made flesh, newly askew.

For the hell of it John-Joe
snaps honeysuckle twigs,

pulls fuchsia stamens out
to stop flowering. His tailor

pins hold flight back,
wings of bees he catches

off guard. When not
sharpening lawn mower

blades, he cuts hedges
and locks off kids who find

sleep's a stranger after he puts
new bulbs in. Trickling *3-In-One*

into small spaces is his forte,
muffles sounds in the dead

of night in this sacred place
our Lord has led him to.

The Book of Bees

> Where the bee sucks, there suck I
> In a cowslip's bell I lie;
> There I couch when owls do cry.
>
> WILLIAM SHAKESPEARE
> *The Tempest*

i

Deep in the depths
of respectability

behind high Palace
walls, snowdrops

'n' daffodils show
early, like women

with child. For
the love of God

to stave shame
from their doors.

McQuaid's army
send baptismal

names from all
parishes to his

Chancellery amidst
wild hellebore.

Clusters of solitary
Christmas 'n' Lenten

roses surprise late
Winter 'n' early Spring.

ii

And the Chancellery's
apiarist collects honey

like money. A broker
of beeswax, combs

and royal jelly
pollenates a retail

trade in rise and fall
of his copperplate hand

to ecclesiastical ledgers
he commends little

people born
outside matrimony

to nibbed elegance
upon his Book of Bees.

He creates hive-ledgers,
lists names and birth

as if carpenter bees,
whose patron saint

is d'face of Lady Lavery.
Enough Hazel's ensure

Godparents identity
hides from adoptees

for good of their
ignorance, word

is according to
the Archbishop's apiary.

iii

A sink doubles
for a font. Invisible

Godparents utter
Baptism after

Fr. Glennon
marks the cross

on my brow, pours
water over my crown,

opens white man
sized handkerchiefs

all five pounds
of me wears,

rubs olive oil
to my breast, lets

his lit *Rothmans*
serve as a candle

in Nurse Gallagher's
soap dish, at her private

Nursing Home.
In consideration

of Lady Laverys
Fr. Glennon's marriage

of sweet balsam
ointment 'n' oil of chrism

seals gifts from
his Holy Spirit, again

at Confirmation
under a brand new name.

Promises invisible
Godparents make

from the Apostles
Creed are Faustian.

Official registry
the Book of Bees

suggests, velvet
sunk by mitre

and crosier
in the presence

of frankincense
as the apiarist

copperplate amends
certificates for fees.

Exclusive fee simple
for St. Patrick's Guild

from Archbishop's
Parish of St. George

in the year of our Lord
Nineteen Sixty-Five.

The Price of 1965, near Archbishop Palace

Under November's wet darkness you enter
Drumcondra's tree-lined respectability, push

in a low sliver gate towards St. Joseph's
fanlight guiding you up its diamond aisle

like a nave to this red bricked three story
Georgian door nurse Gallagher opens. Lets

night in and the one you carry day 'n' night
for nine months to this anaglyptic hallway,

narrow as a birth canal, dimly lit shadows
climb walls, little by little, beyond return

to a top box room. Do you lift the sash
window, let the outside in, or not come

out till I leave your womb, hurting as if
the man who left half the idea of me.

Roses ramble your wallpaper incarceration,
traces branches that do not match

like how this came to pass, and the unlikely
bonds that will betray. And as your waters

break your pelvic floor widens what
will be given up, what'll not be talked

of becomes clear, as I appear crown first
under the eye of the sacred heart's red light

into the hands of nurse Gallagher, who
cuts our cord, (according to a well buried

birth certificate up in Werburgh Street); who
hands me over for a fist full of Lady Laverys

rolled up in a black velvet band like a Roman
candle, to a nun in a Hillman making for the ferry.

Finding Myself in Werburgh Street

In the diocese of Dublin and Glendalough
up along Dame Street, past the Olympia

and Dublin Castle, in earshot of Christchurch
bells, Werburgh Street Church stands above

Lord Edward Fitzgerald's vault, atop of
Swift's baptismal font, not a stone's throw

from where birth and death records lie,
like coordinates to be plotted, half-truths

waiting to be lies on deValera
and McQuaid's map of cardinal truths.

I take down oversized red bound birth
books for 1965 in the records room,

turn pages heavy with births from Skull,
Mizen and Hook Heads to Sheep's Hollow

beyond boarder crossings, flyover latitudes,
boreen longitudes and oyster beds where sand

and grit form pearls under blatherwrack,
an irritant stuck inside the oyster's body

swaying to salt making free with buoyancy
around the Ring of Kerry and Cliffs of Moher

as I run my finger across districts and parishes:
Annagor, Belmullet, Cahir, and Drumcondra

the Swine of Pigs, in the diocese of Clonturk
where real fiction lives. Though not the Book

of Kells, it illuminates a pentimento of fibs,
stretching back to the foundations of belief.

Not five minutes shy of two hours I lean into
a past of myself, as unrecognisable as a wild

pearl, iridescent and luminous as the shell itself
or my fingerprint smudged. Reading my birth

name given is like a foreign language forged
in copperplate, a kind of twisted mother-tongue

as if finding the needle, without eye or haystack,
purposefully sent to hit a dead end by the grace

and blessings of the Archbishop's handmaidens.
Without Theseus thread of Adriane, nurse Gallagher

cuts the chord, registers me by her own hand,
every slope and ink incline a natural fabrication

of this twenty-six year old's maiden name, who
didn't comfort me as my first tooth breaks through,

hold me at night as my breath is given over to
coughing for the loss of you, or watch me not fall

down as one foot follows the other in a gait you'd
half recognise disappearing into a crowd years later.

Instead you commend me into the geometry of a life
you'd not foresee. All the while, wondering from a distance.

Bellybutton

Do you wish
you'd gone

for a backstreet
job above

in Hatch Street,
or not been

caught off guard
in the first

place. Instead
this secret

birthing house
confines us.

Corner sink exposes
its pipes below

the Blessed Virgin
into the heart

of which a blunt
knife sits

betraying
my afterbirth

in a room where
a two-bar fire

glows into this night,
nurse Gallagher

pulls me out of you,
into a world

of unknowing.
My first breath-cry

clouds windows,
lines my lungs

with a dampness
my breathing

will carry like
the pain of arrival

and your departure
into thin air

born like the memory
of mist falling

on bracken,
suspending disbelief,

my innie pit
our belly to belly

chord leaves,
is all that

remains
of our attachment.

False Start

Conceived over a gallon of gin
in a room the Lafranchini Brothers

would die for and others later
kill for a thread of the sin made

flesh under intricate stucco work
of who knew what, rises in relief

fifty years on as word breaks
a good likeness is found not far

from the scene of the crime.
I am three hours as the crow flies

undetected for decades. The spit
of you cannot be denied.

Yet truth-drops rub against lies,
aggregates bound by secrecy

hardens as if lime, till I show up
falling through water like stone.

Finding You at Fifty

Fifty years ago it was inconceivable
for you to think I'd find you, having written

a stranger's name in your place, before
giving me up. On the back of a throwaway

remark your name surfaces. Archives split
the wind to offer you up, gives chance

its photographic way, as you look
from a parochial landscape out at me.

Something in a trick of light betrays
our line of beauty, different but the same.

What with a similar left shock of white hair
I know I am of you. See my own reflection

look back at me for near the first time,
sure in the knowledge of what's in a name.

Multiplicity

Your chaste respectability
is taken advantage of,

caught-out by forced
persuasion, I imagine.

In giving you the benefit
of doubt, my naïveté

shines, like afterbirths
you expel with natural

ease, here and there.
Bear earlier and later

mutations of myself
into being. Doesn't cost

you a thought, making
free with your charms

like bracelets jettisoned
to a nuns sale of work.

You begin again
via ferry. A fast-girl upon

high Seas, who fails
to look back.

Our histories
diverge to collide

as I unearth
irrefutable truths

that survives
like land breaking waves.

Districts Not Apparent

For best results
fast twenty-four

hours beforehand.
With the head

of a lolly-pop stick
I scrape internal

cheek cells
into a sterilised vial.

Add saline solution
'n' shake like a daiquiri.

Seal and send.
Wait for a lab

to pick percentages
hidden in ethnicity.

A dolly-mixture
result reveals

the sum of my parts.
I am of Ireland.

European. British
Isles. Iberian. Ashkenazi.

I share trace elements
from Siberia, Western

Middle East,
Asia Minor and South

Central Africa.
Yet, I am of Ireland

carrying the wealth
of geographies histories.

IV

A Mother's Love a Blessing
No matter where you roam
Keep her while she's living
You'll miss her when she's gone

    Thomas Peter Keenan
    A Mother's Love a Blessing

Requiem for the Sold

i. *Entrance*

Fifty years ago a stranger
carries all five pounds of me

over the threshold. Leaves me
high 'n' dry to the mercy of nuns.

I go back, up granite steps,
through peacock green doors

the width of my arms tell
it's nine fifteen at a stretch.

Over hand painted tiles I glide
past panelled doors that closed

deals, drawn by light through
the entrance hall archway, past

alcoves saints held a child
to their chest under Osborne's

stucco work. Holy water fonts
and sacred heart lights frame

architraves as if stamps on letters
to; Idaho, Ohio, Colorado, Oregon,

Hawaii, Mississippi, or Wisconsin
fall on doormats. Faces under

two years old, stare back
at strangers offering a better life

complete with refrigerator
and yard. Before the rot sets in

or a gardener's dog retrieves
small bones under wisteria.

Before neglect and weather
takes hold at Temple Hill,

exchanges occur after Civil
Servants affix infant-photos

to Irish passports, allows
Éire's babas sell over

Seas from a Free State
sans Mothers' consent

often, outlay invoices
due attached.

New parents settle
nuns balance sheets.

ii. *Attic Stairway*

Cobwebs feign indifference.
Walls narrow. The ceiling

lowers as I pass fourteen
faded frame-marks

where Stations hung.
The first cartoons babies

see over a nun's shoulder.
With my palm on the same

short banister, I step up.
A high altitude corridor

runs wind the length
of this Georgian, I can

almost touch clouds
reading blueness

nearer my God
to thee echoes from

rooms to thrive
or die in. Before salmon

paint peels away,
pigeon droppings matt

feathers, or light
refusing darkness enters

rooms cots sat proud
as if *Mothercare*.

After sales price-tags
ensures a lifetime

of gratefulness
is fully paid up.

   iii. *Attic Floor*

Caught in the gap time creates
under nun's feet, over and back

across decades, linoleum grows
thin as a communion wafer. Once

lifted, wide floorboards offer up
a pattern of souls who trod not

in the dead of night to ease
infants' pain of abandonment but

counts Harp 'n' Hen, Rabbit
'n' Greyhounds into Munster

and Leinster paper coin bags:
pounds, shillings 'n' pence fall

as if indulgences into their
Silvermines of half-crowns,

sovereigns 'n' guineas stacked
like a Blackjack banker.

Thousands in small change
under foot, could fill Keeper Hill

full o' thru'penny bits, florins
and rolls 'n' rolls of ten bob notes.

A bank for the dispossessed
wrapped up in torn sheet music.

A Mother's Love a Blessing
holds rows of 1965 pennies

no matter where you roam
skyscraper-tall beneath boards.

Soul of my Saviour echoes
into afternoons, fledglings

flock to open mouthed
fireplaces, nest in grates

fires burnt fevers from
in the parish of Monkstown

in the barony
of Dún Laoghaire-Rathdown.

*Love her as in childhood
Though feeble old and grey
For you'll never miss your mother's love
Till she's buried beneath the clay.*

—Thomas Peter Keenan
A Mother's Love A Blessing

Save The Child

38628   ST. PATRICK'S GUILD
and ST. PATRICK'S INFANT HOSPITAL & NURSERY COLLEGE (Incorporated)
TELS.: BLACKROCK 258   DUBLIN 44691
(FOUNDED 1919 WITH THE APPROVAL OF HIS GRACE THE ARCHBISHOP OF DUBLIN)
Central Office—50 MIDDLE ABBEY ST., DUBLIN
'PHONE 44531

6 . 12 . 1935

Received of *Miss O' Éire*

the Sum of £3-0-0

being a *il Baby O' Éire* to the Society.

S. J. Xaveria
on behalf of the Local Committee.

NOTES ON POEMS

Advocaat is a Dutch alcoholic beverage made from eggs, sugar and brandy. Similar to eggnog in its smooth custard-like flavour and richness.

Archbishops of Dublin from 1852-2017:

1852-1878	Paul, Cardinal Cullen
1879-1885	Edward, Cardinal MacCabe
1885-1921	William Walsh
1921-1940	Edward Byrne
1940-1971	John Charles McQuaid CSSp
1971-1984	Dermot Ryan
1984-1987	Kevin McNamara
1988-2004	Desmond, Cardinal Connell
2004-present	Diarmuid Martin

Archbishop John Charles McQuaid (1895-1973) was Archbishop of Dublin and Primate of Ireland 1940-1971. Also referred to in these poems as: Charlie, J.C. or McQuaid.

Ashurst later renamed **Notre Dame des Bois** by Archbishop John Charles McQuaid was the property and environs he resided at in Killiney, County Dublin. Travelling daily by one of his chauffeur driven cars to the official residence at Archbishop Palace/House in Drumcondra, Dublin 9.

Babycham was launched in Britain in1953 as a sparkling Perry. It was directly marketed for women as an affordable alternative to Champagne.

Black and Tans were officially the Royal Irish Constabulary Special Reserves. They were recruited during the Irish War of Independence, and later became infamous for their attacks on civilians and their property.

Crème de Menthe Frappés are a mint or peppermint flavoured alcoholic beverage.

Earl of Clonmel (1739-1798) aka Copper-faced Jack. John Scott was the1st Earl of Clonmel, known as Lord Earlsfort between 1784-1789, Viscount of Clonmel from 1789-1793. He was an Irish barrister and judge serving as Lord Chief Justice of the King's Bench for Ireland from 1784 to 1798.

Cruice, M.J. (1860-1951) Mary Josephine Cruice was born in Galway. She was the foundress of St. Patrick's Guild in 1910, and served as Honouree Secretary of St. Patrick's Guild until 1943, when the Sisters of Charity replaced her at Archbishop J.C. McQuaid's behest. In 1928 M.J. Cruise took a 500 year lease on Neptune House, Temple Hill. She moved her already established St. Patrick's Hospital and Infant Hospital from 39 Mountjoy Square in the city of Dublin to Neptune House, Temple Hill, Monkstown, County Dublin.

Dear Frankie (1922-1993) Frankie Byrne was Ireland's first RTÉ radio agony aunt from 1963-1984.

Sr. Denis/Mother Denis (1906-2002) was a Religious Sister of Charity who hailed from Newport, Co. Tipperary. She was associated with and ministered at St. Patrick's in Kilkenny, St. Vincent's Elm Park, and Linden/Talbot Lodge Convalescent Home (1944-1997). Sr. Denis/Mother Denis also administered Archbishop John Charles McQuaid's household at *Notre Dame des Bois*, Killiney, County Dublin until his demise in 1973.

Éamon de Valera (1882-1975) was an Irish politician from 1917-1973 who also served as President of Ireland for 14 years. He was close associate of Archbishop John Charles McQuaid. He convalesced at Linden/Talbot Lodge. Also referred to in these poems as Dev.

Fee Simple is the greatest possible estate in land. It represents absolute ownership of land.

Francini Brothers/Lafranchini Brothers were eighteenth century Swiss Stuccodores.

A Great Fall this poem owes a debt to the nursery rhyme *Humpty Dumpty*.

Harbour Hotel was an RTÉ radio soap drama. It aired at lunchtimes from 1975-1990.

The Holy Land was a colloquialism for Archbishop John Charles McQuaid's residence at *Notre Dame des Bois* in Killiney, County Dublin.

Imogen Stuart RHA (b.1927-) is a German-Irish sculptor. Predominately known for her religious sculptures. She lives in Sandycove, County Dublin.

Keeper Hill is a hill in Foilduff, north County Tipperary.

Kiskadee rum was a trademark for Irish Distillers Ltd.

Lady Lavery was a painter and the second wife of the celebrated portrait artist Sir John Lavery. Her likeness appeared on Banknotes of Ireland for much of the 20th century.

McArdles was an Irish red ale brewed in Dundalk.

Moher Clé is a mountain in north County Tipperary.

A Mother's Love's A Blessing is an Irish folk song written by Thomas Peter Keenan (1866–1927).

The Mulkear is a river that flows through Counties Limerick and Tipperary.

Neptune House was once the Earl of Clonmel's summer residence. Later it was used as a holding pen for illegitimate children to be sold from. Operated by the Religious Sisters of Charity on behalf of Archbishop John Charles McQuaid.

Patrick Osbourne was an Irish Stuccodore.

Ramsay Hunt's Syndrome causes facial shingles. This condition can cause ear pain, facial paralysis, loss of taste and hearing.

Recidivist means "to fall back." Commonly used to discuss the relapse rate of criminals, who have served their sentence and have been released. However, in the poem *Mrs. Doogan* it exemplifies the Religious Orders usage of the word to describe women who fell pregnant on more than one occasion.

Rennie, Sir John (1761-1821) a Scottish engineer appointed Aird as acting engineer at Howth Harbour/Pier, Custom House Dock and Kingstown Harbour/Dún Laoghaire Piers.

The River Saile...Weila, Weila, Waile is an Irish children's nursery rhyme. This type of song is called a Murder Ballad or Child Ballad, named after Francis James Child. He was the first person to catalogue these types of songs, prior to his death in 1896.

Rothmans is the brand name of a British tobacco manufacturer. Founded by Louis Rothman in 1890 as a small Fleet Street, London kiosk.

Saudade is a Portuguese word for the love that remains after someone is gone.

Shaws is the trading name of an Irish retail store.

Sheanafork is a mountain in north County Tipperary.

Soul of My Saviour is an Irish Folk hymn about the Eucharist. It is an English paraphrase of the 14th century Latin prayer, Anima Christi, first published with the tune ANIMA CHRISTI, written by the English Jesuit priest William Joseph Maher in 1864.

Show Me the Way to Go Home is a popular song written in 1925 by James Campbell and Reginald Connelly after a train journey.

Spangle(s) was a brand of boiled sweets manufactured by Mars Ltd., 1950-1980s.

St. Patrick's Guild was founded by M.J. Cruice in 1910. Over the years the Guild has moved from Ranelagh, Abbey Street, Haddington Road and finally to 203 Merrion Road. The Guild's motto was *Save the Child*. M.J. Cruice remained Honouree Secretary until 1943, when the Sisters of Charity replaced her at Archbishop J.C. McQuaid's behest. St. Patrick's Guild is a registered Adoption Society with a Charity status number of 7562.

St. Patrick's Infant Dietetic Hospital & Nursery College In 1928 M.J. Cruise took a 500 year lease on Neptune House, Temple Hill. She moved her already established St. Patrick's Hospital and Infant Hospital from 39 Mountjoy Square to Temple Hill, Monkstown. The Hospital was operated by the Religious Sisters of Charity until the late 1980s.

3-In-One is a multi-purpose household lubricant for small items things that squeak.

Vicks is an American brand name of over-the-counter medications, e.g. Vicks Vapour-Rub.

Werburgh Street houses the General Register Office of Irish Genealogy Records (GRO).

A SELECTION OF SOURCES CONSULTED

ARCHIVES

Butte-Silver Bow Public Archives

Dublin City Archives (DCA)

General Register Office of Irish Genealogy (GRO)

Irish Architectural Archive (IAA)

The National Archives of Dublin (NAI)

National Library of Ireland (NLI)

New York Newspaper Archives 1753-2017

The Valuation Office Ireland

Registry of Deeds

BOOKS/ARTICLES/ PERIODICALS

Adie, Kate, *Nobody's Child* (Hodder Headline, London, 2006).

Arendt, Hanna, *The Human Condition* (UCP, Chicago, 1958).

Bellew, Séamus, *Coats of Arms and the Bellew Family* (Co. Louth Archaeological and Historical Society), *Journal of the County Louth Archaeological and Historical Society*, Vol. 25, No. 4 (2004), pp. 426-450.

Boland, Eavan, *Object Lessons, The Life of the Woman and the Poet in our Time* (London, Vintage, 1996).

Browne, Noël, *Against the Tide* (Dublin, Gill & Macmillian, 2007).

Butler, Sr. Katherine, RSC, *Neptune on the Temple Hill* (Dublin Historical Record, Vol. 39, No. 31986, pp, 98-107 and F.E. Ball, *A History of County Dublin: the People, Parishes and Antiquities from the Earliest Times to the close of the eighteenth century*, 1902, Part First, pp. 18-19.

Casey, Christine, *Making Magnificence: Architects, Stuccatori, and the Eighteenth-Century Interior* (Yale, University Press, 2017).

Clarke, Austin, *In Austin Clarke: Selected Poems*, ed. W.J. McCormack, "Living in Sin," & "Unmarried Mothers," pp.65-66, (London, Penguin, 1991).

Chambers, Anne, *T.K. Whitaker: Portrait of a Patriot* (London, Doubleday Ireland, 2014).

Coogan, Tim Pat, *De Valera: Long Fellow, Long Shadow* (London, Hutchinson, 1993).

Cooney, John, *John Charles McQuaid, Ruler of Catholic Ireland* (Dublin, O'Brien, 2009).

Corless, Damien, *The Greatest Bleeding Heart's Racket in the World: Irish Hospital Sweepstakes* (Gill & McMillan, Dublin, 2010).

De Breffny, Brian, *The Lafranchini Brothers, Irish Arts Review* (1988), pp.212-221.

Goulding, June, *The Light in The Window* (Dublin, Poolbeg, 1999).

Humphreys, Margaret, *Empty Cradles* (London, Corgi, 2011).

Kay, Jackie, *The Adoption Papers* (UK, Bloodaxe, 2013).

Kay, Jackie, *Red Dust* (UK, Picador, 2011).

Kennedy, Teresa, Sister Stan, *The Road Home: My Journey* (London, Transworld Ireland, 2011).

Lapotaire, Jane, *Everybody's Daughter, Nobody's Child* (London, Virago Press, 2007).

Mac Cormaic, Ruadhán, *The Supreme Court* (London, Penguin Ireland, 2016).

Mac Sheahan, J. J. "St. Patrick's Guild." *The Irish Monthly*, vol. 71, no. 843, 1943, pp. 357–365. www.jstor.org/stable/20515175.

Milotte, Mike, *Banished Babies* (Dublin, New Island, 2012).

O'Brien, Conor Cruise, *IRELAND* (London, Andre Deutsch Ltd., 1969).

O'Sullivan, Eoin, & Raftery, Mary, *Suffer the Little Children* (Dublin, New Island, 1999).

O'Sullivan, Michael, *Seán Lemass: A Biography* (Dublin, Blackwater Press, 1994).

O'Reilly, Seán, *Irish Arts Review: Patrick Osbourne, An Irish Stuccodore, 1989-1990*, pp.119-126.

O'Riordan, Steven, *Whispering Hope, The True Story of the Magdalene Women* (London, Orion, 2015).

Palmer, Caitríona, *An Affair with My Mother* (Penguin Ireland, Random House, 2016).

Pearson, Peter, *Of Sea & Stone: Paintings 1974-2014* (Cork, Gandon Editions, 2014).

Pearson, Peter, *Between the Mountains and the Sea* (Dublin, O'Brien Press, 1998).

Raftery, Mary, *Do They Think We're Eejits? A Selection of Irish Times Columns 2003-2009* (Dublin, Irish Times Publications, 2013).

Rivlin, Ray, *Jewish Ireland: A Social History* (Dublin, History Press, 2011).

Robinson, Mary, Robinson, Tessa, *Everybody Matters: A Memoir* (London, Hodder & Stoughton, 2012).

Sissay, Lemn, *Gold From Stone* (London, 2016).

Smith, James M, *Ireland's Magdalen Laundries and the Nation's Architecture of Containment* (Indiana, University of Notre Dame Press, 2007).

Taylor, Anne, *A Spool of Blue Thread* (London, Chatto & Windus, 2015).

Verrier, Nancy Newton, *The Primal Wound: Understanding the Adopted Child* (Baltimore, Gateway Press, 2015).

Whelan, Gerard, & Swift, Caroline, *Spike: Church-State Intrigue and The Rose Tattoo* (Dublin, New Island, 2002).

LEGISLATION

The Adoption Acts (Dublin, Stationary Office) 1952, 1964, 1974, 2010.

The Adoption (Amendment) Bill (Dublin, Stationary Office) 2016.

The Adoption (Information and Tracing) Bill (Dublin, Stationary Office) (2015).

Communications Regulation (Amendment) Act (Dublin, Stationary Office) 2007.

Constitution of Ireland (Dublin, Stationary Office) 1937.

Criminal Law Amendment Act (Dublin, Stationary Office), 1935.

Criminal Justice Act (Female Offenders Bill) (Dublin, Stationary Office), 1942.

Criminal Justice Act (Dublin, Stationary Office), 1960.

The Code of Canon Law of the Catholic Church (Dublin, Stationary Office) 1983.

Dance Halls Act (Dublin, Stationary Office) 1935.

The Easter Proclamation of the Irish Republic (Dublin, Stationary Office) 1916.

Guardianship of Infants Act (Dublin, Stationary Office) 1964.

Infanticide Act (Dublin, Stationary Office) 1949.

Legitimacy Act (Dublin, Stationary Office) 1931.

Registration of Maternity Homes Act (Dublin, Stationary Office) 1934.

Status of Children Act (Dublin, Stationary Office)1987.

Succession Act (Dublin, Stationary Office) 1965.

CASE LAW

GM; FM v TAM [1972] 106 ILTR 82 (High Court, Kenny, J).

Keegan v Ireland 18 EHRR 342 [1994]: Adoption: Child born out of wedlock.

I.O'T v B, I R. [1989] IR 321, Adoption Law: The Case for Reform.

Johnston v Ireland (A/112) [1986] 9 EHRR 203.

McGee v. Attorney General [1974] IR 284.

Open Door and Dublin Well Woman v Ireland (A/246) [1992] 15 EHRR 244.

Roe v. Wade, 410 U.S. 113 [1973].

The State (Nicolaou) v. An Bord Uchtála [1966] IR 567.

W. O'R v. EH [1996] 2 IR 248.

REPORTS/OTHER

Adoption Law: The Case for Reform. The Law Society's Law Reform Committee Report, April 2000.

Report into the History of Adoption in Ireland since 1922: Sean Ross Abbey, Castlepollard, & Bessborough, Mother & Baby Homes, July 2013; Compiled by the members of Adoption Rights Now, with cooperation, assistance and support from the members of Beyond Adoption Ireland and Open all Adoption Records Now.

The Carrigan Report 1935 [The Criminal Law Amendment Act 1935].

Committee on Evil Literature Report, (Dublin, Stationary Office) 1927.

Department of Local Government and Public Health Annual Report (Dublin, Stationary Office) 1932-1933.

Inter-Departmental Group on Mother and Baby Homes, Department of Children and Youth Affairs Report, July 2014.

The Kennedy Report [The Reformatory and Industrial Schools System Report, 1970].

The Murphy Report 2009.

Law Reform Commission Report on The Hague Convention on the Law Applicable to Succession to the Estates of Deceased Persons (1989), [LRC 36-1991].

MAPS

The Glucksman Map Library at Trinity College, Dublin.

Ordnance Survey Ireland.

NEWSPAPERS

Albuquerque Journal, Anaconda Standard, Anglo Celt, Billings Herald, Boston Globe, Cavan Times, Chicago Tribune, Clare Champion, Connacht Tribune, Corkman, Derry People, Donegal Times, Dundalk Argus, Dungarvan Observer, Evening Echo, Evening Press, Farmer's Journal, Financial Times, Freeman's Journal, Galway Independent, Guardian, Idaho Statesman, International Herald Tribune, Irish Examiner, Irish Independent, Irish Times, Irish Press, Kerryman, Las Cruces Sun-News, Las Vegas Review-Journal, Leitrim Observer, Limerick Leader, Meath Chronicle, Messenger, Montana Post, Munster Express, Nationalist, Nenagh Guardian, New York Post, New York Times, Nevada Appeal, Pensacola Journal, Pittsburgh Post-Gazette, San Diego Union, Sarasota Herald-Tribune, Seattle Times, Sunday Independent, Sunday Times, Telegraph, The Tablet, Tipperary Star, Tipperary Voice, Tuam Herald, Wall Street Journal, Washington Post, Wexford Echo, Youghal Tribune.

A SELECTION OF SEMINAL NEWSPAPER ARTICLES

Barbash, Fred, *'The 'mother and baby home' at Tuam, Ireland, where friends just 'disappeared, one after the other,'* The Washington Post, March 13th, 2017.

Bingham, John, *'Cardinal's apology to mothers over babies handed over for adoption,'* The Telegraph, November 3rd, 2016.

Bracken, Amy, *'Opinion: Adoption, illegitimate children and 'the bogey of proselytism' in Catholic Ireland,'* The Journal.ie, June 29th, 2014.

Brennan, Cianan, *'Sold to the highest bidder' – how Ireland's Institutions allowed Americans to adopt Irish children in the 1950s,'* The Journal.ie, January 9th, 2017.

Brown, Helen, *'Jackie Kay Interview,'* The Telegraph, October 31st 2016.

Buckmaster, Luke, *'Women of the stolen generations: 'I want my story out,'* The Guardian, November 28th, 2016.

Carolan, Mary, *'Supreme Court to hear appeal over foreign adoption recognition,'* Irish Times, March 30th, 2017.

Clarke, Donald, *'Why do we still broadcast angelus bongs?'* Irish Times, March 18th, 2017.

Cooney, John, *'Retired priest can now pick up pension,'* Irish Independent, November 13th, 2008.

Cooney, John, *'Adopted child's religion McQuaid's main concern,'* Irish Times, March 18th 1996.

Costello, Norma, *'Mass graves in Ireland: A long history of Church abuse,'* Aljazeera.com, March 27th, 2017.

Donnelly, Rebecca, *'13 year old girl and her Twin Babies buried in Roscrea,'* written from the Broadcast on Midlands 103, March 2017.

Doyle Higgins, Erica, *'We knew our babies would be sold to the highest bidder'* — Irish woman tells of son 'left to die' in mother and baby home,' Irish Post UK, Mach 8th, 2017.

Ferriter, Diarmaid, *'St. Vincent's was built with public money,'* Irish Times, April 3rd, 2017.

Finlay, Fergus, *'We should take a moment this Christmas to mourn children who died alone in Mother and Baby Homes,'* Irish Examiner, December 22nd, 2015.

Finn, Christina, Enda Kenny to face questions over Tuam revelations: *'No nuns broke into our homes to kidnap our children — we gave them up,'* Journal.ie, March 7th, 2017.

Ferguson, Donna, Lemn Sissay: *'My foster patents were good people who did bad things'*, The Guardian, September 30th, 2016.

Hanley, Valerie, *'Illegally Adopted Woman's Plea for help to find the Irish Mum she never knew,'* Extra.ie, March 19th, 2017.

Henry Lee, *'Standing up for Fallen Women,'* Theatre Review of *Madame Geneva* by Jo Egan, The Sunday Times, May 7th, 2017.

Irish Examiner, *'Commission won't say if it contacted adoption authority on report dealing with illegal birth registrations'*, April 19th, 2017.

Irish Examiner, *'State accused of misleading United Nations on Magdalen liability,'* April 10th, 2017.

Irish Examiner, *'Bessborough survivor demands Government excavate the site for human remains'*, March 20th, 2017.

Irish Examiner, *'Philomena Lee 'appalled' at Tuam revelations'*, March 17th, 2017.

Irish Examiner, *'Giving up a child for Adoption has a lifetime impact'*, September 16th, 2008.

Irish Times, *'In 1974 I drove myself to the Cork mother and baby home'*, March 18th, 2017, (author anonymous but known to the paper).

Irish Times, *'Boy passed off as couple's 'natural child', mother says'*, May 7th, 2016.

Irish Times, *'Ambitious Plans for Georgian House and Apartments Conversion in Blackrock,'* May 21st 2015.

Journal.ie, *'A Life Unlived: 35 years of slavery in a Magdalen Laundry,'* Samantha Long's account of her mother Margaret Bullen, who died in Gloucester Street laundry aged 51.

Kelly, Dara, *'Catholic League Bill Donohue's shameful personal attack on Tuam babies hero Catherine Corless,'* Irish Central.com, April 7th, 2017.

Kelly, Fiach, *'Government alarm at possible redress for mother and baby home victims,'* Irish Times, March 23rd, 2017.

Kenna, Colm, Case Studies: *'Adopted son won landmark case after being left out of will,'* Irish Times, April 25th, 2016.

Kenny, Mary, *'Revisiting illegal adoption cases,'* The Irish Catholic, September 26th, 2013.

Langan, Sheila, *'Death records for 796 children at Tuam home published in full,'* Irish Central.com, June 17th, 2014.

Laskow, Sarah, *'The Invisible Unmarried Mothers of Ireland'*, Atlas Obscura, March 16th, 2017.

McCahill, Elaine, *'The Sisters of Our Lady of Charity want to build a new convent and extend a nursing home at the site of a former Magdalene laundry in north Dublin,'* July 28th, 2014, Herald.ie.

McCarthy, Justine, *'Call for genocide prosecution over mothers' homes,'* The Sunday Times, April 9th, 2017.

McCarthy, Justine, *'I idolised my big sister, but society cast her out when she got pregnant,'* The Sunday Times, March 19th, 2017.

McCarthy, Justine, *'Justice is priceless for these mothers,'* The Sunday Times, April 16th, 2017.

McCarthy, Justine, *'Bishop says new hospital must obey the church,'* The Sunday Times, April 23rd, 2017.

McConnell, Daniel & Ó Cionnaith, Fiachra, *"Seize Church lands to pay for abuse,"* says Government.' Irish Examiner, March 13th, 2017.

McGarry, Patsy, 'RTE to screen 'Dear Daughter' documentary tonight: Highly influential programme recalls childhood of the late Christine Buckley,' Irish Times, April 7th, 2014.

McGarry, Patsy, 'Church Marks 40 years of defending its message,' Irish Times, November 5th, 2015.

McGarry, Patsy, 'Sisters of Charity to be given new National Maternity Hospital,' Irish Times, April 18th, 2017.

Milotte, Mike, 'The baby black market,' Irish Times, June 28th, 2014.

Minihan, Mary, Power, Jack, Burns, Sarah, 'Maternity hospital will 'respect rights of the mother', nun says,' Irish Times, April 20th, 2017.

Murray, Sean, *"I wasn't shocked, I knew there were there"*: Catherine Coreless *receives standing ovation on Late Late,'* The Journal.ie, March 10th, 2017.

O'Brien, Tim & McGarry, Patsy, 'Leo Varadkor says Government 'Cannot seize Church Lands', Irish Times, March 12th 2017.

O'Connell, Jennifer, 'I am haunted by the Tuam babies, what would they have become?', Irish Times, March 15th, 2017.

O'Connor, Mary, 'Access to Files for Tuam Baby Home a 'basic right,' says TD,' Galway Advertiser, March 16th, 2017.

O'Dowd, Niall, 'Tuam Babies: "It would be...kinder to strangle children at birth," doctor said,' [re: Dr. Ella Webb's comments on illegitimate children, June 18th 1924], Irish Central.com, March 6th, 2017.

O'Dowd, Niall, 'Tuam: The dreadful night the parish priest came for an unmarried pregnant girl,' Irish Central.com, March 12th, 2017.

O'Faolain, Aodhan, 'Tusla opposing man's claim for Tuam baby information,' Irish Times, April 18th, 2017.

Ó Fátharta, Conall, 'In Search of a long lost boy,' Irish Examiner, April 19th, 2010.

Ó Fátharta, Conall, 'Excluded agency 'aware of illegal birth registrations', Irish Examiner,' April 13th, 2015.

Ó Fátharta, Conall, 'No Appetite to uncover scale of illegal adoption scandal,' Irish Examiner, April 13th, 2015.

Ó Fátharta, Conall, 'Fears over 'trafficking' of children to the US,' Irish Examiner, June 3th, 2015.

Ó Fátharta, Conall, *'Centre and Laundry 'one and the same,'* Irish Examiner, June 4th, 2015.

Ó Fátharta, Conall, *'Failure to honour Magdalene promise,'* Irish Examiner, August 26th, 2015.

Ó Fátharta, Conall, *'Brothers united after spending eight decades apart,'* Irish Examiner, August 28th, 2015.

Ó Fátharta, Conall, *'Angel Plot' in Tuam surveyed,'* Irish Examiner, October 10th, 2015.

Ó Fátharta, Conall, *'Women seek inclusion in Laundry Redress Scheme,'* Irish Examiner, October 13th, 2015.

Ó Fátharta, Conall, *'Bessborough Mother and Baby Home: Order reported 80 more infant deaths to State than were on death register,'* Irish Examiner, November 9th, 2015.

Ó Fátharta, Conall, *'HSE knew of 'quasi illegal' Bessborough Adoptions in 2011,'* Irish Examiner, December 16th, 2015.

Ó Fátharta, Conall, *'Mother and Baby Homes: Plenty of information about Adoption records to be found if State wishes to look,'* Ó Fátharta, Conall, Irish Examiner, December 3rd, 2015.

Ó Fátharta, Conall, *'HSE knew of 'quasi illegal'* Bessborough Adoptions in 2011, Irish Examiner, December 16th, 2015.

Ó Fátharta, Conall, *'Nuns told not don't co-operate as Bishop tried to thwart probes into Bessborough scandal,'* Irish Examiner, November 23rd, 2015.

Ó Fátharta, Conall, *'St. Patrick's Guild sought €50k from Tusla for Adoption Records,'* Irish Examiner, October 18th, 2016.

Ó Fátharta, Conall, *'Bessborough:We have a right to know the truth,'* Irish Examiner,' November 15th, 2016.

Ó Fátharta, Conall, *'Bessborough Mother and baby vaccine trial files altered,'* Irish Examiner,' November 15th, 2016.

Ó Fátharta, Conall, *'Vaccine trials: Unravelling the drug trials scandal,'* Irish Examiner, November 17th, 2016.

Ó Fátharta, Conall, *'Vaccine trial victim to lodge complaints over altered file,'* Irish Examiner, November 17th, 2016.

Ó Fátharta, Conall, *'Vaccine changes inquiry urged,'* Irish Examiner, November 18th, 2016.

Ó Fátharta, Conall, *'Religious orders rebuffed funding requests for Magdalene women redress,'* Irish Examiner, 'March 14th, 2017.

Ó Fátharta, Conall, *'Ministers raised ears of Magdalene redress cost in 2011,'* Irish Examiner, March 27th, 2017.

Ó Fátharta, Conall, *'Mother and baby homes' redress ruled out by Cabinet,'* Irish Examiner, April 12th, 2017.

Ó Fátharta, Conall, *'Mother and Baby Homes report misses the mark,'* Irish Examiner, April 13th, 2017.

O'Grady, Eileen, *'Account of the retirement of former Temple Hill nurse,'* Knockdown News: source: Presentation Sisters news website. No date given.

O'Halloran, Marie, *'Christian Brothers papers show children being 'sold into slavery,''* Irish Times, March 23rd, 2017.

O'Halloran, Marie, *'Dáil to debate call for truth commission on mother and baby homes,'* Irish Times, March 19th, 2017.

O'Loughlin, Ann, *'Woman sues over alleged forced adoptions in 1969,'* Irish Examiner, February 10th, 2016.

O'Morain, Padraig, *'Adoption agency's misinformation is blamed for years of fruitless searching,'* Irish Times, April 8th 1997.

O'Neill, Aliah, *'The Legacy of Church-run Mother and Baby Homes in Ireland,'* Irish America, August/September 2010.

O' Sullivan, Claire, *'Sisters of Charity received legacy money,'* Irish Examiner, June 27th, 2011.

O'Toole, Emer, *"The Catholic church is 'shocked' at the hundreds of children buried at Tuam. Really?'* The Guardian, March 7th, 2017.

O'Toole, Emer *'The Sisters of Charity presided over abuse. They must not run a maternity hospital,'* The Guardian, April 20th, 2017.

O'Toole, Fintan, *'Ireland is still defined by the church's mindset,'* Irish Times, March 2017.

Palmer, Caitríona, *'No returning to 'normal' life for women after giving up baby,'* Irish Independent, July 22nd, 2013.

Rooney, Caoimhe, *'The history of forced adoption in Ireland,'* The Circle, February 26th, 2015.

RTE.IE. – no author accredited to the Tom Wall story, *'Former industrial school inmate wants documents archived or public,'* April 12th, 2017.

Sherwood, Harriet, *"Catholic church apologies for role in 'forced adoptions' over a 30-year period,'* The Guardian, November 3rd, 2016.

Smith, James M, *'Ireland's forgotten diaspora – banished unwed mothers and adopted babies,'* Irish Central, March 23rd, 2017.

Sweeney, Tanya, *"My birth mum was told to get rid of me or she couldn't go home' – How new legislation can change everything for Irish adoptees,'* Independent.ie, November 30th 2016.

Tierney, Ciaran, *'Tuam babies adopted in large numbers to US, says historian who broke the scandal,'* Irish Central.com, March 26th, 2017.

Tierney, Ciaran, *'How she did it: the heroic Irish historian who broke the Tuam baby scandal,'* Irish Central.com, March 25th, 2017.

Walshe, Sadhbh, *'Suffer the Little Children: Church Cruelty in Ireland,'* New York Times, March 30th, 2017.

Wayman, Sheila, *"I don't have a Single Piece of reliable information about who I am.' Barnardos course for Adopted adults explores the complex emotions on all sides,'* Irish Independent, October 5th, 2015.

PRIVATE INTERVIEWS

Margo Bellew, former SSL and of Annagor House.

Cherry Coogan, friend of Archbishop John Charles McQuaid.

Sr. Eileen Fahey, RSM, Founder of Aiséire.

Lorraine Harte, Nursery Nurse at St. Patrick's Infant Dietetic Hospital & Nursery College, Temple Hill, Monkstown, in the 1980s.

Fr. Paddy Jones, parish priest of St. Columbus, Iona Road, Dublin 9.

Monsignor Tom Stack, former member of the Catholic Communication Office and RTÉ Radharc documentary team.

RADIO

Adoption: Marie McLoughlin was a Pan Am airhostess in the 1950s who transported an 18 month old Irish baby to America by prior arrangement. Live Line, RTÉ Radio 1. Broadcasted March 15th, 2017.

Adoption / Mother and Baby Homes. Live Line, RTÉ Radio 1. Broadcasted March 14th, 2017.

Adoption / Mother and Baby Homes: St. Rita's Private Nursing Home, Sanford Road & Illegal adoptions. Live Line, RTÉ Radio 1. Broadcasted March 13th, 2017.

Catherine Corless: the historian who unearthed the Tuam Babies Scandal. BBC Radio 4. Broadcasted March 25th, 2017.

Childhood Adoption: Journalist Justine McCarthy & her long lost nephew Duncan Carr on Marian Finucane Show. RTÉ Radio 1. Broadcasted March 25th, 2017.

Interim Report Into Mother and Baby Homes Published. RTÉ 1. Susan Lohan, Co-founder of Adoption Rights Alliance (ARA). Today with Sean O'Rourke. Broadcasted April 11th 2017.

Mothers and Daughters: A story of Adoption. RTÉ DOCUMENTARY ON ONE Archive (1994). Broadcast March 11th, 2009.

McNeice, Stephen, *'We have a long way to go before there's a real separation of church and state,'* SEAN MONCRIEFF News Talk, Broadcast May 13th, 2017.

Los Precroso: A story of Adoption. RTÉ DOCUMENTARY ON ONE Archive. Broadcast June 21st 2011.

Ray Darcy Show: Cathy Lee former Nursery Nurse at St. Patrick's Infant Dietetic Hospital & Nursery College, Temple Hill, Monkstown, in the 1970s. RTÉ Radio 1. Broadcast March 27th, 2017.

Ray Darcy Show: Noeleen Ennis Hickey & Anne Fitzgerald discuss St. Patrick's Infant Dietetic Hospital & Nursery College, Temple Hill, Monkstown, and St. Patrick's Guild in 1965 & 1972. RTÉ Radio 1. Broadcast April 3rd, 2017.

Ray Darcy Show: Adoption Stories. Teresa Tinggal & Sharon Lawless of Adoption Stories. RTÉ Radio 1. Broadcast April 20th, 2017.

A Servant of God: Archbishop of Dublin and Primate of Ireland between December 1940 and February 1972. DOCUMENTARY ON ONE. RTÉ Radio 1. Produced by Denis O'Grady. First broadcast on June 17th 1973.

TangledWeb. Part 1. The History of Adoption in Australia. RTÉ DOCUMENTARY ON ONE Archive. Broadcasted February 2014.

TangledWeb. Part 2. The History of Adoption in Australia. RTÉ DOCUMENTARY ON ONE Archive. Broadcasted February 21st 2014.

Twenty-Fifty Anniversary Retrospective on John Charles McQuaid, April 1998. Produced by John Bowman, April 1998.

A Pocket of Time. The Other Side of the Adoption Story. News Talk FM. Broadcast April 10th, 2014. Produced by Susan Dennely.

Philomena Lee and her daughter Jayne Libberton on Tuam Babies revelations. TODAY WITH SEAN O'ROURKE. Broadcast RTÉ 1, March 15th, 2017.

How valuable are Adoption life story books? BBC Radio 4, YOU AND YOURS. Broadcast August 5th, 2015.

Who's the Daddy? BBC Radio 4 World Service, OUTLOOK WEEKEND. Broadcast October 2nd, 2016.

Why is Temple Hill excluded from the commission of inquiry into the Mother and Baby Homes? TODAY WITH SEAN O'ROURKE, RTÉ 1. Brian O'Connell interviews Anne Fitzgerald, on St. Patrick's Guild's exclusion from the Mother and Baby Home commission of inquiry and Claire McGettrick of Adoption Rights Alliance (ARA) on The Clann Project, Broadcasted October 24th, 2016.

TELEVISION/FILM

Adoption Stories. Produced by Sharon Lawless of Flawless Films. Broadcast TV3. Series, 2014, 2015, 2016, 2017.

Altered State. Broadcast on RTÉ 1, October 2005.

A Secret Buried: The Mother and Baby Scandal/Tuam Mother & Baby Home. CLAIRE BYRNE LIVE. Broadcast RTÉ 1 on, March 6th, 2017.

The Boys of St. Vincent. A two part docudrama based on events at Mount Cashel Orphanage in St. John's Newfoundland. Directed by John N. Smith for the film board of Canada, 1992.

Britain's Adoption Scandal: Breaking the Silence. Produced by Ronachan Film. Broadcast on UTV/ITV, November 9th, 2016.

Catherine Corless, the Galway historian that discovered the Tuam Babies mass grave. Interview on the LATE LATE SHOW. Broadcast on RTÉ 1, March 10th, 2017.

Cardinal Secrets, a Prime Time special. Produced by Mary Raftery and reported on by Mick Pelo. Broadcast on RTÉ 1, 2002.

Dear Daughter, examined childhood experiences of the late Christine Buckley others at Goldenbridge orphanage. Produced by Louis Lentin. Broadcast on RTÉ 1, February 22nd 1996.

Examination of Illegal Adoptions by Commission Ruled Out. RTÉ 1 News report by Joe Little. Broadcast July 27th, 2016.

Ireland's Lost Babies Documentary. Produced by Martin Sixsmith. BBC2 Broadcast September 17th, 2014.

Paula Douglas: Search for the Truth. St. Patrick's Guild 1959. Illegal registration birth. No legal records exist. Broadcast on THE LATE LATE SHOW, RTÉ 1 May 27th, 2017.

Primetime: Bessborough Mother & Baby Home which provoked an investigation in the 1940s – How many children died and were buried there. Reporter, Rita Coogan. Broadcast on RTÉ 1 April 4th, 2017.

The Radharc Squad. A two part documentary examining the role of the religious programme Radharc from 1962-1996 in Irish Broadcasting. First established under Archbishop John Charles McQuaid 1959. This series was broadcast in 2012 on RTÉ.

Separation of Church & State. Broadcasted on CLAIRE BYRNE LIVE. Amnesty International's Colm O'Gorman & David Quinn of the Iona Institute. Broadcasted on RTÉ 1, March 13th, 2017.

Secrets & Lies. Movie about adoption & trace. Written and directed by Mike Leigh, 1996.

States of Fear, a three-part documentary series examined the abuse of children in residential institutions in Ireland. Produced by Mary Raftery. Broadcast on RTÉ 1, 1999.

Woman Loses Adoption Case against Religious Order. RTÉ 1 News report October 21st 2015.

THEATRE

Postscript. Written by Noelle Brown and Michélle Forbes. This is a story about an adoptees search for identity. Features Noelle Brown and Bríd Ní Neachtain. Director and Production designed by Conor Hanratty. Staged at The Abbey's Peacock Theatre, June 14th-24th, 2017.

ACKNOWLEDGEMENTS

During the course of writing *Vacant Possession* I have had the good fortune to encounter a myriad of organisations and their individuals on a variety of occasions, some of whom are acknowledged, others wished to remain anonymous. Therefore I wish to express my gratitude to all and to the following.

At Adoption Rights Alliance (ARA), to Susan Lohan, Kathy Finn & Claire McGettrick; Andrew Walker at Barnardo's Post Adoption Services; Department of Foreign Affairs; Galway Archaeological and Historical Society (GAHS); Grand Lodge of A. F.& A. Masons of Ireland; Huguenot Society of Great Britain and Ireland; Irish Georgian Society (IGS); Yvonne O'Connor at the Irish Jewish Museum; Sharon Lawless at Flawless Films; County Louth Archaeological and Historical Society; Millmount Museum, Drogheda.

At the Religious Sisters of Charity Adoption Society St. Patrick's Guild, I should like to thank the Director of Services Sr. Francis I. Fahy RSOC, and Archivist Sr. Monica Byrne RSOC; Adoption Authority of Ireland (AAI); Ireland's national Health Service Executive (HSE); Access Industrial and Related Records (AIRR); Freedom of Information Officers at the Health Service Executive (HSE); Tusla Adoption Services; Temple Street Children's University Hospital.

I would like to acknowledge staff at the General Register Office Roscommon, Northern Ireland, England, Scotland, Wales & New York. And In particular to all at the Research Room in the General Register Office of Irish Genealogy (GRO), Werburgh Street, Dublin 2. In addition to the staff at the Registry of Deeds, Henrietta Street, Dublin 1.

Equally I should like to acknowledge Abraxas; Angela & John Bellew; Geraldine Brennan; Valerie Dennison; Jimmy Duffy; Aileen Gaughran-Katkib; Martha Woodcock; Kate Hickey; Bernie O'Donnell; Dolores Quinlan; Helen Walsh and Sharon Woods for the gift of friendship.

And for granting me permission to wander freely in the abandoned Neptune House building at Temple Hill whilst under construction (September 26th, 2016), I am enormously grateful to Gerry

McGreevy and Liam Wealdon of Crosswaithe Developments/New Generation Homes Limited. They exhibited more humanity and Christian kindness than many so called religious people I encountered during the course of writing *Vacant Possession*.

Should you have crossed the threshold at Neptune House, Temple Hill, Monkstown, County Dublin, as an adoptee and wish to make contact with me, you may do so at this email address: templehill-monkstown@gmail.com

Author Postscript

That good things happen out of adversity is a truism I have come to embrace on foot of the avalanche of unimaginable revelations and events that were to unfold subsequent to my beloved Parents' demise, giving way to a schism not seen since Luther nailed his decree to a door. And in so doing would irrevocably alter the shape of my familial landscape forever.

On the international stage post-Independence Ireland purports to be an all-inclusive open society, yet it is not without luminous contradictions. Namely, the theory that socioeconomic and political progress has lead us out of the claustrophobic religiosity of the deValera-McQuaid era, which in my opinion is a pure notional one. Outwardly some window dressing has changed but ostensibly little has altered. A pale imitation of engagement is employed by the authorities when pressed, whilst a more robust dismissive lip-service is paid to those attempting to ascertain what lies beneath. Thus a disingenuous spin permeates whilst firmly embodying the deValera-McQuaid ethos and its firm hold on our Nation.

From engagement with various State and Church agencies together with research conducted I can confirm that Éire's Architecture of Containment thrives in matters pertaining to the release of Adoption Records in Twenty-First Century Ireland. A trinity of control and culpability pervades within the Catholic Church, the Irish Free State and its Religious Institutions specifically established to contain, to profit from and to manage the lives of those who bore children outside marriage and the little lives born outside of the bands of holy matrimony.

I would assert that incongruities exist whilst the vicissitudes of historical events remain static.

Compliance and Poor Practice are conveniently ushered in as scapegoats, whilst legislation endeavours to straightjacket those seeking answers. Cannon Law still supersedes Common Law in matters pertaining to the release of Adoption Files and related records in Ireland. I have found in certain instances the authorities choice of approach to be one of threefold.

(1) To obfuscate behind loosely framed selected legislation.

(2) To ignore written requests for files and or information.

(3) To claim no records exist — where persistence has proven this to be untrue.

In cases where records do exist they are often incomplete, scant or incorrect.

For instance in my particular case I was seeking all my medical records from 1965-1967, for the first 565 days whilst under the care of the Religious Sisters of Charity from the Health Board now the HSE, in an attempt to glean knowledge of those missing 18 months; and also to ascertain if I had a predisposition to any respiratory conditions I was unaware of. As I had developed a chronic recurring respiratory condition after my Mother's demise in 2013.

In 2015 I initially sought all my medical information under a Freedom of Information and Data Protection Acts requests. In the Health Service Executive's Business Manager's letter of July 27th, 2015 quoting from Section 15 (1) (a) of the FOI Act that "...the record concerned does not exist or cannot be found...." and continues that the "HSE Dublin South does not hold Child/PHN/Immunisation records as far back as 1965/1967. The Administrator for the area has confirmed that these records would have been destroyed i.e. confidentially shredded." He further states "if any records from 1965/1967 within the scope of your request existed, they would have been disposed of in this process."

In 2016 Temple Street Children's University Hospital confirmed in their December 6th, 2016 letter that "although we have located the index card, we have unfortunately been unable to locate [your] healthcare Record." The index card – states dates of admission and departure dates for two separate occasions in 1966, but proffers no medical reason or details for same.

Notwithstanding in a telephone conversation to a member of the Risk Management Department on March 9th, 2017 they confirmed paper medical records existed dating back to 1965/1967 and that a manual search for same could be conducted. Once again on March 11th, 2017 I wrote to Temple Street Children's University Hospital reiterating my request and advising them of our telephone conversation. On April 6th, 2017 I received scant medical information from Temple Street Hospital. In some instances with half the photocopied pages missing, rendering details incomprehensible. On foot of which a series of correspondence ensued. May 3rd, 2017 I wrote again, on this occasion expressing my dissatisfaction at their complete lack of dignity and respect in not furnishing a Full Facsimile of All Medical Records as requested. Given that I have seen Full Facsimiles of Medical Files for others who attended Temple Street Hospital before and after 1965. The Hospital's reluctance to release my medical files seems odd.

On May 5th, 2017 Temple Street Hospital reissues the same scant information contained in their April 6th, 2017 correspondence, providing an enhanced version from the microfilm.

Contained amongst it is a letter of April 18th, 1967 from Dr. D. McHale at St. Patrick's Hospital at Temple Hill, to a Dr. J. Mac Auliffe Curtin in Temple Street Children's Hospital. Dr. D. McHale refers to both myself and another child on the same one page letter, not affording us the curtsey and best practice of individual letters. Whilst Temple Street's records accredit no individual date of birth, choosing instead to record the term I Year Old. The medical practitioners neglect in not treating each child as an individual, smacks of a profound sense of indignity. Not to mention an unethical medical practice not to afford each patient with their respective medical file.

This same Temple Street Children's University Hospital Report, accredits an Incorrect Blood Group to me. On endeavouring to obtain clarification as to whether an Incorrect Blood Group has been accredited or is this in fact my medical file at all? They state in their May 30th, 2017 letter "…microfilmed Healthcare Records cannot be amended…" clearly choosing to obfuscate and ignore my question and initial request, not to mention the gravity of their medical negligence. This seems somewhat anomalous with their assertion in the same letter that, "The hospital prides itself on treating patients, former patients…with dignity and respect at all times…" I cannot help but wonder would a child who had not passed through the gates of Temple Hill to Temple Street Children's Hospital be treated with such a lack of dignity and disrespect, or indeed be subjected to such unethical discrimination whilst endeavouring to obtain their Medical Records?

In 2015 I wrote via registered mail to The Archbishop of Dublin, Dr. Diarmuid Martin seeking my original Baptismal Certificate. To date he has neglected to acknowledge or respond to my letter. As a devout and practicing Catholic I am astounded by his indifference. Given the words of his address at the 22nd Consultation Day for Diocesan Communications Offices at All Hallows College, May 6th, 2015 where he stated:

"It is important always to stress that all children, whatever the circumstances of their birth, should be loved unconditionally and treated with the same rights and dignity. This applies also to their rights within the Church."

The fundamental disregard and subservient manner in which many of these organisations have exhibited towards me may be construed as nothing short of a basic infringement of Human Rights. And reiterate, would a child who had not passed through the gates of the Religious Sisters of Charity St. Patrick's Guild at Temple Hill to Temple Street Children's University Hospital, St. Columbus Church and Archbishop Palace be treated with such blatant distain, indifference and lack of human dignity, whilst endeavouring to obtain their Medical and Baptismal records? Thus raising questions as to why the brute force of transparency is so shy to reveal itself? Why does a deep rooted vein for lack of love for transparency prevail? Might Indemnity not be at the heart of matter?

Notwithstanding the aforementioned, it makes sense now why I have been graced with an innate appreciation for Eighteenth Century Georgian Architecture and imbued with an acute sensibility for its Stucco work, surely a throwback from my first 565 days at Neptune House.

I have had the opportunity to meet some remarkable people in the most likely circumstances along the way. Each of whom greeted me with an unconditional openness, a selfless willingness to give of themselves and their time through their virtuous encouragement in a steadfast manner — which is deeply refreshing in this current age, where certain sectors appear to have made little gods of those favouring to build their houses, brick by avaricious brick upon mendacious ley lines.

For those who have guided me — without question their shared thread was that of the rather unfashionable yet hugely underrated attribute of **Kindness**, all of which has helped nudge me toward the Truth. And know it is I who is deeply privileged to have made their acquaintances and all the more enlightened and enriched to have discovered that

> it is in the small gestures of kindness
> we give to one and other
> that true humanity is to be found —

ANNE FITZGERALD
Dún Laoghaire
Fall 2017

Author Photograph © Therese Aherne

ANNE FITZGERALD was raised in Sandycove, County Dublin. She is a graduate of Trinity College, Dublin and Queen's University, Belfast. Her poetry collections are *Swimming Lessons* (Wales, Stonebridge, 2001), *The Map of Everything* (Dublin, Forty Foot, 2006) and *Beyond the Sea* (Co. Clare, Salmon Poetry, 2012).

In 2006 Anne founded Forty Foot Press, in addition to two School Publishing Houses, Monkstown Educate Together Press (MET Press, 2003) and Loreto Abbey Dalkey Press (LAD Press, 2004). She is a recipient of the Ireland Fund of Monaco Writer-in-Residence bursary at The Princess Grace Irish Library, Monaco. She teaches Creative Writing in Ireland and North America. Anne lives in Dún Laoghaire, County Dublin.

For biography visit Forty Foot Press at www.fortyfootpress.com/anne-fitzgerald.html and on Facebook see www.facebook.com/FortyFootPress.2006/

"Like the sea-run Steelhead salmon that thrashes upstream to its spawning ground, then instead of dying, returns to the sea – Salmon Poetry Press brings precious cargo to both Ireland and America in the poetry it publishes, then carries that select work to its readership against incalculable odds."

TESS GALLAGHER